Educators a

Educators as First Responders is a comprehensive, hands-on guide to adolescent development and mental health for teachers and other educators of students in grades 6-12. Today's schools are at the forefront of supporting adolescents with increasingly complex, challenging psychosocial needs. Moreover, students are more likely to seek out a trusted teacher, advisor, or coach for support than to confide directly in a parent or even a school counselor. Succinct and accessible, this book provides tips and strategies that teachers, coaches, nurses, counselors, and other school professionals can put into immediate use with students in varying degrees of distress. These evidence-based practices and real-world classroom examples will help you understand the "whole student," a developing individual shaped not just by parental pressure or psychiatric diagnosis but by school and broader cultural and systemic forces.

Deborah Offner is a Clinical Psychologist who has worked in schools and colleges as a counselor, educator, and consultant for 25 years. She is Consulting Psychologist at Beacon Academy in Boston, MA, and provides counseling, supervision, and professional consultation to several other middle and secondary schools. Her areas of expertise include adolescent development and mental health, student affairs, and professional development for K-12 educators.

Other Eye on Education Books
Available from Routledge
(www.routledge.com/k-12)

**Learner Choice, Learner Voice: A Teacher's Guide to
Promoting Agency in the Classroom**
Ryan L Schaaf, Becky Zayas, and Ian Jukes

Supporting Student Mental Health: Essentials for Teachers
Michael Hass and Amy Ardell

**The K-12 Educator's Data Guidebook: Reimagining Practical
Data Use in Schools**
Ryan A. Estrellado

**Teaching as Protest: Emancipating Classrooms
Through Racial Consciousness**
Robert S. Harvey and Susan Gonzowitz

**The Brain-Based Classroom: Accessing Every Child's
Potential Through Educational Neuroscience**
Kieran O'Mahony

**The Media-Savvy Middle School Classroom: Strategies
for Teaching Against Disinformation**
Susan Brooks-Young

Educators as First Responders

Responders

A Teacher's Guide to Adolescent Development and Mental Health, Grades 6-12

Deborah Offner

Routledge
Taylor & Francis Group
NEW YORK AND LONDON

Designed cover image: © Shutterstock

First published 2023
by Routledge
605 Third Avenue, New York, NY 10158

and by Routledge
4 Park Square, Milton Park, Abingdon, Oxon, OX14 4RN

*Routledge is an imprint of the Taylor & Francis Group,
an informa business*

ISBN: 978-1-032-05914-3 (hbk)
ISBN: 978-1-032-41607-6 (pbk)
ISBN: 978-1-003-35892-3 (ebk)

DOI: 10.4324/9781003358923

Typeset in Palatino
by SPi Technologies India Pvt Ltd (Straive)

To Sam – my most loving, enthusiastic supporter
To Julia – my favorite middle, high school, and college student

Contents

Meet the Author

Deborah Offner, a clinical psychologist, has spent twenty-five years in schools and colleges as a classroom teacher, counselor, administrator, and consultant. She also maintains an active clinical practice, where she works with adolescents and their families.

Dr. Offner spent fourteen years as Consulting Psychologist and, subsequently, Dean of Students, at an independent high school in Boston. Currently, she serves as Consulting Psychologist to Beacon Academy, a one-year, full-time program that prepares highly motivated students from communities with limited resources to succeed in competitive high schools. Dr. Offner also supervises school counselors, consults to school leaders, and provides professional development to educators and educational content to parents about adolescent development and mental health.

Dr. Offner holds a B.A. from Wesleyan University and a Ph.D. from Boston University. She lives in the Boston area with her husband and daughter.

Introduction

Not long ago, I was on the phone with the assistant head of a New Jersey boarding school. I was providing an employment reference for a colleague being considered for Dean of Students. In giving me an overview of the position, the Assistant Head explained, "The thing is, in this job, every year there are situations where a student walks in and tells you something you've never, ever heard before." I burst into laughter. Not because this was funny, but because it succinctly conveyed the kind of truth that someone who's never worked in a school would not imagine, but anyone who has worked in a school for more than a couple of years probably takes for granted.

The problems that drop onto administrators' laps tend to be the most pressing or complex. But we would do well to remember that those same difficulties first made themselves known in a classroom, on the playing field, or in the office of a teacher, coach, or adviser.

As a clinical psychologist, I've spent the past twenty-five years working in and collaborating with the institutions that educate—and care for—our kids. I do this because classrooms hold a certain magic for me, due to my own experience of growth within them, as well the engagement and growth I observe in the students I teach and counsel.

When I began my career as a psychology professor at a state university, I noticed that my English department colleagues tended to find themselves with crying students in their offices more than they (or I) would have expected. The tears wouldn't have to do with difficult assignments or disappointing grades, but rather personal issues, such as break-ups, arguments with friends, or feelings of not fitting in. My colleagues were not sure why or how they kept ending up in this situation, why students chose them to confide in.

But once I thought about it, it made sense. Students felt comfortable with their English professors in part because they delved into personal material while writing for their classes. Also, the students regarded them as smart, caring adults—who were *not* a psychologist, physician, or a parent. Students saw them as wise, but more in a literary sense than a medical or authoritarian one. In other words, to many students, English professors make perfect confidantes.

When I moved on to become a school counselor at an independent secondary school, I noticed that, once again, teachers were the go-to for students—though this population wasn't partial to their English teachers. They confided in faculty members they liked and trusted, no matter their discipline.

Sure, some kids sought me out, as did their parents, but most of my "referrals" came from teachers. Sometimes they wanted to bring to my attention a student who had confided in them about a stressor, loss, or mental health issue. Other times, teachers came to me directly after noticing a student was distracted, irritable, withdrawn, or somehow "different" from their usual self during class, lab, or on a field trip.

These teachers were perceptive, thoughtful, and compassionate people. Most would be the first to say they didn't know how to address the wide range of developmental and emotional issues that their students presented them with. That's where I'd come in. Often, I could simply suggest some things my colleague could say or do, and they would take it from there. Other times, the teacher and I would arrange a meeting between me and the student. Sometimes, the student, for their own comfort, would bring their teacher or advisor to our initial meeting.

Within months of becoming a school counselor, I recognized that teachers were my eyes and ears, a primary referral source, and my closest allies in supporting our students. About midway through my fourteen years at that school, I came to conceive of educators as "First Responders" to students' emotional tribulations.

Today, in my private practice, where I continue to specialize in adolescents, I routinely hear about students' favorite teachers: those they admire, those they want to please, those they feel understand and care about them. It's not unusual for my patients to confide in a trusted teacher about their parents' divorce or a sexual assault, as well as about intellectual interests or career aspirations.

As a middle- or high-school teacher, you, like me, spend your time with pre-teens or teenagers. You engage with them as they are going through normal adolescent development, which even under the best of circumstances can be confusing and tumultuous. You also bear witness as they experience loss, trauma, and emotional and material hardship. When something goes wrong, it often shows up at school first.

Nothing in formal teacher education can quite prepare you to judge what's happening when a student encounters difficulty or presents in a different or concerning way. Is the student just being a "typical" teen or is something more afoot?

I wrote this book to call attention to the pivotal role middle- and high-school educators play in the growth and development of our adolescents—not just academically but emotionally as well. I also wrote it give educators—or "First Responders"—insight into the inner lives of the teenagers you work with daily, so you can become even more confident in guiding your students toward adulthood.

To give educators the information that will be most useful, I've structured the book in three parts. Each part focuses on a different aspect of the forces that shape the adolescent perspective and how you—the educator—can put those forces to work in your classroom and in your everyday interactions with students.

Part one—Educators and Adolescents—takes a deep dive into the inner dynamics at work in the adolescent mind. It considers the emotional challenges, thought patterns, and developmental tasks of middle- and high-school-aged students and their related behaviors. Within this section's chapters, you learn what's going on for your students developmentally, what to expect (and what not to expect) from them cognitively and behaviorally, how to manage what is likely to come your way, and how to recognize when professional attention is needed

In part two—Social Contexts—the chapters address the larger social forces—race, ethnicity, culture, socioeconomic class, gender identity and sexual orientation, and crisis—that shape our students' experiences, identities, and thinking as they work so hard to define themselves. Each chapter provides clear explanations of the "force" it addresses, the pressures that force may create, and how both you and your school can take these forces into consideration when responding to students.

Part three—Strengthening Their Circle of Support—explains that educating a teenager is not a solo task. It takes a village to usher a child successfully through middle school and high school. This section lays out how to cultivate your particular "village" of parents, colleagues, and even school policy to support your students and yourself. It then shows you how to use that team to build an emotionally healthy school for everyone.

Each chapter ends with a vignette that is a composite of situations I've encountered in the schools where I've worked and consulted. The vignette is followed by a short list of discussion questions designed to help you explore the information found in the chapter and see how you might put it to use in your classroom—and maybe even use it to create school policy. While you can go through each exercise by yourself, I encourage you to recruit a few colleagues, read the book together, and then go through the exercises as a group.

My hope for this book is that it gives renewed confidence in shepherding your students toward adulthood and realizing their dreams, even through these difficult times. The insights gained here can guide you in demystifying adolescent behavior, shaping classroom practices to better connect with adolescent minds, and improving school policies around mental health and wellbeing. But perhaps most comforting, you'll be better prepared to identify troubled behavior in a student before it becomes serious or life changing. Better yet, you'll know exactly what to do about it.

Section I
Educators and Adolescents

1

Educators as First Responders

I'm not trained for this!

– Ninth-grade science teacher

You teach high school English. Kevin, a thoughtful, artistic tenth grader, approaches you with a question about the current assignment. He appears more tired than usual, even a little disheveled. Because you know him fairly well, after you answer his question, you ask, "How are things going?"

He looks down for what seems like a long time. When he raises his head, there are tears in his eyes. "Not great," he says.

"Is something wrong?"

Kevin hesitates. Then, in an almost inaudible voice, he says, "My parents are separating."

You're taken aback by this news. Your heart goes out to Kevin. But behind him, your second period students are filing into your classroom and taking their seats.

Your next class starts in seven minutes.

DOI: 10.4324/9781003358923-2

Or let's say you teach at a middle school and coach their girls' basketball team. One night, after your team has grabbed another win—thanks in large part to a thirteen-year-old star player Josie—two other girls on the team, Addie and Mia, approach you.

"Coach, you have to promise not to tell," Addie says. "Josie would kill us if she found out we told you. She made us promise not to say anything to her parents or anyone at school."

As the lump in your throat grows, you look both girls in the eye. You promise nothing. Addie continues anyway, "We noticed scratches on Josie's legs while we were in the locker room. And we know she's been watching TikToks where teenagers talk about cutting themselves."

"They make it sound cool," Mia chimes in.

You don't say a lot because, honestly, you're not sure how to respond. You thank the girls for bringing this to your attention, assure them they've done the right thing, and fumble for your phone. As they walk away, you see the time glowing on your screen. It's 10 p.m.

If you've taught, coached, or cared for students in middle or secondary school, I suspect neither of these scenarios surprises you. You and your colleagues have likely had these kinds of exchanges (some less dramatic, some more so) with your own students. In these moments, part of you is relieved that the student turned to you when they found themselves in over their head. And truth be told, you may be somewhat flattered a student trusted you with their problems.

However, part of you may be uncomfortable. You haven't been formally trained to deal with the complex psychosocial issues many of your students face. You don't feel competent responding to such matters on your own. You rightly wonder where the boundaries are or should be, and most of all, you worry you could do more harm than good.

As a clinical psychologist specializing in adolescent and mental health—and a consultant to middle and secondary schools across the United States—I am acutely aware of this conundrum. Educators who work with adolescents are increasingly on the front lines of a national adolescent mental health crisis. You're not the only one. Your middle- and secondary-school colleagues—whether in public, independent, faith-based, mainstream, or special-education settings—share your instinct to help students, along with your anxiety, even trepidation, about doing so.

Chalk It Up to Adolescence

Even without distinct psychological, social, or economic challenges or stressors, middle- and high-school students face a daunting task: growing up. Right around sixth or seventh grade, as part of entering puberty (a biological phase) and adolescence (a psychosocial phase), your students begin their physical, intellectual, and emotional transition from childhood to adulthood—a transition that will busy their bodies and minds for more than a decade. As all of us know (in part from having gone through it ourselves), this phase of growth presents a host of challenges and conflicts for the adolescent and everyone in their lives, including their teachers.

One of the more significant brain-based changes of adolescence occurs in an area called the prefrontal cortex. This brain region is responsible for complex cognitive behaviors (e.g., reasoning, decision-making, problem-solving, self-awareness). As the prefrontal cortex develops, students are able to comprehend and generate more complex ideas. This is what makes teaching sixth and seventh graders so exciting. You get to witness the proverbial light bulb going off in their heads as they grasp abstract concepts for the first time.

However, like all other changes during this developmental phase, this doesn't happen overnight. In fact, the prefrontal cortex doesn't typically reach full functionality until around the age of twenty-five. Until then—and certainly during middle and high school—students' brains are essentially construction sites. The circuitry is spotty at best and cannot be counted on. While they sometimes reason well and produce mature thoughts, more often than not they can't, so don't. Teenagers aren't yet in full control of their thinking or themselves. This is why teenagers are famous for rash decisions and social "drama."

Picture yourself trying to get through a day full of perplexing tasks, complicated interpersonal relationships, confusing societal messages, and competing demands without your highly evolved reasoning, decision-making, impulse control, and interpersonal skills, and you get a sense of what your students are up against.

School Is Their World

Of course, adolescents' construction site of a mind comes to school with them. And school—like no other area of their life—fires that hobbled circuitry to full capacity, both intellectually and socially.

For most adolescents, their world is school-centric. School is where tweens and teens spend most of their time. It's where their work (learning) is. It's where their peers are and where their relationships happen. It's also where their parents aren't, so school is where they begin to shape their individual identities and, with any luck, begin to figure out for themselves how to deal with life's demands and problems.

Starting around age eleven or twelve, students are increasingly aware of their own strengths and weaknesses—academically, athletically, artistically, socially, and physically. They naturally compare themselves to others and look to their peers for approval and acceptance.

Complicating this process is the fact that each student is moving through these physical and cognitive changes at their own pace. Just as a full range of heights as well as facial hair is on display throughout middle- and high-school hallways, various stages of cerebral and psychological development are evident, if not as obvious.

Each student is judging whatever happens in class—or at lunch, or on the athletic field—from their own developmental vantage point. As you might imagine and have likely experienced, this unevenness in comprehension and reasoning (not to mention self-awareness and self-regulation) leads to misunderstandings and miscommunications among students. Unevenness across students may fuel disagreements and heighten emotions, leading to hurt feelings or worse harms. Remember, however mature they may appear, your students' logical reasoning and impulse control are not necessarily ready for what the environment demands of them.

In the academic realm, a student whose brain is maturing at an average rate might have no trouble adjusting to the new rhythms of middle school. But a student whose brain is maturing more slowly faces a multitude of challenges. As they wait for the cognitive capability to plan, organize, and follow through to come on board, such students find typical middle-school experiences—such as changing classrooms, juggling the expectations of multiple teachers, and taking courses that require more complex comprehension skills—difficult, if not impossible.

There are also numerous psychosocial discrepancies across students that show up in middle school. For example, some sixth and seventh graders already have romantic interests, while other students don't show this kind of interest until high school or even college. A student can be perfectly healthy and normal anywhere along this continuum. However, due to disparities in "pace" in this area, students who have been close friends for years can find themselves in pretty different places socially. Understandably, this can be crushing and incomprehensible for the student who feels left behind.

During adolescence, a day can feel like a week and a week can feel like a day. There is so much to learn and manage, but most adolescents don't yet have the mental and emotional capacity to think it all through, let alone generate the kind of competent response we (and they) would like.

Once students arrive in high school, their attention spans, for one thing, do increase. However, they don't always focus this greater span in the most productive direction—at least not to our adult way of thinking. With a backdrop of pulsing hormones and persistent social pressures, high-school students are preoccupied by myriad issues.

When the choice is between academics or their peers, as you well know, their peers may take priority. Never is this truer than when a friend is in distress. Generation Z adolescents (born after 1997) are more attuned to not only their own moods, anxieties, and "ups and downs," but also to those of their close peers. A 7th grader recently told me that when a friend tells her they are having a tough day or dealing with a difficult issue, she makes a note in her phone so she is reminded to check in with them on subsequent days, to see how they're doing. Another example: I recently got the following text message from a twelfth grader, canceling our weekly therapy session. "Can't meet today. Friend in crisis." At school, student may think nothing of missing something important—for example, your class—to comfort a struggling friend.

Another pressing psychological factor for adolescents is social comparison. They are developmentally driven to compare themselves to others and compete for peer approval. On any given school campus, you can see this express itself in ways reflective of the institution's culture. At some schools, you see it in the way students dress. At others, students one-up each other with clever quips in class. And in still others, athletic prowess or artistic ability are how students win popularity and the acceptance that comes with it. While this is not a new phenomenon among teenagers, it's even more intense and unrelenting for this generation because of social media, the ultimate social comparison accelerator.

Finally, the primary developmental task of adolescence is achieving emotional independence from parents or guardians. Complicating this push toward individuation is the fact that middle and high schoolers still need mature guidance—and they know it. Every minute of every day, your students are navigating a world and a way of perceiving a world that is in constant flux for them.

Nowhere do the challenges and various aspects of adolescence development surface more profoundly or play themselves out more fully than at school—where you, their teacher, are (in effect and fact) the only adult in the room. Thus, when a student needs an adult, not surprisingly, you become their natural choice.

"I'm Not Trained for This!"

As one panicked teacher so aptly shouted into the phone as she solicited my advice about responding to a student in crisis, "I'm not trained for this!"

I'm pretty sure you didn't exactly sign up for some of this stuff, either. Yet this is the reality of teaching middle schoolers and high schoolers. Though you may doubt you're the best option when it comes to intervening in your student's developmental or personal challenges, your students have no such reservations. That's why they seek you out. They know and regard you as a functioning "adult"—in other words, an expert in all things life.

While you may not feel like an expert in "all things life," and may even have substantial evidence to support your hunch, recognize that in this arena you do offer competencies that other adults simply can't. You have an established relationship with your students—they listen to you, they're interested in what you think. You play a consistent and key role in guiding them toward a promising future. Many times, they don't or won't listen to other adults—least of all, parents.

You are the "boots on the ground" in your school community. Unlike any other adult in your students' lives, you observe them day in and day out in their natural habitat. You not only witness their daily interactions, you also know all the players. In addition, you and your colleagues are typically the first adults to notice when something isn't right with a student—when they seem tired or irritable, are suddenly sitting apart from their friends, or uncharacteristically fail to turn in an assignment.

Do not discount the value of your knowledge when it comes to being a First Responder to adolescent discontent or more serious personal or emotional difficulties. I've mused with more than one teacher or mental health colleague that middle- and high-school teachers today are a lot like "milieu workers" in pediatric or psychiatric care institutions. In these clinical settings, milieu workers are embedded in the institutional environment, or "milieu," where they monitor, support, and assist patients. Their role is not only to administer medications, provide advice, or offer resources, they're there to meet their charges where they are, in the moment.

When I served as a school counselor, and later when I was dean of students at a high school, teachers were my best source for flagging a student in need. And teachers continue to be my closest partners in my consulting work.

When a student comes to you in crisis, you want to be sure your response will be effective and appropriate. Note that this does not require a degree in psychology. With some basic knowledge of adolescent development and strategies for handling the various situations most likely to come your way—all of which you'll find in the following pages—you can feel confident in this dimension of your role, and transform yourself from apprehensive educator to competent First Responder. As an added bonus, you can use what you learn here to further improve your communication with your students and be an even more effective teacher.

Best of all, the next time a student turns to you for help, the lump in your throat will be smaller. You'll know what to say and do. You'll know how to be fully present for your students and help them withstand—and even grow from—the challenges they face as they traverse the winding, pot-hole riddled road of adolescence.

Talk It Out: Scenarios and Questions for Discussion

Below are the two scenarios that began this chapter. Read through each again. Then consider the questions that follow. Better yet, get a group of your colleagues together to talk through these situations using the questions to help you think through your options and argue the pros and cons of various approaches. Use these discussions to better prepare yourself—and your school— for the typical developmental and mental health issues you're likely to encounter.

Once you've read through the entire book, it might be informative to come back to these scenarios and see if your thoughts on handling these situations have changed.

Kevin

You teach high school English. As the bell rings and you watch your students file out of your classroom, Kevin, a thoughtful, artistic tenth grader, approaches you with a question about the current assignment. He appears more tired than usual, even a little disheveled. Because you know him fairly well, after you answer his question, you ask, "How are things going?"

He looks down for what seems like a long time. When he raises his head, there are tears in his eyes. "Not great," he says.

"Is something wrong?"

Kevin hesitates. Then, in an almost inaudible voice, he says, "My parents are separating."

You're taken aback by this news. Your heart goes out to Kevin. But behind him, your second period students are coming in and taking their seats.

Your next class starts in seven minutes.

Josie

You teach at a middle school and coach their girls' basketball team. One night, after your team has grabbed another win—thanks in large part to a thirteen-year-old star player Josie—two other girls on the team, Addie and Mia, approach you.

"Coach, you have to promise not to tell," Addie says. "Josie would kill us if she found out we told you. She made us promise not to say anything to her parents or anyone at school."

As the lump in your throat grows, you look both girls in the eye. You promise nothing. Addie continues anyway, "We noticed scratches on Josie's legs while we were in the locker room. And we know she's been watching TikToks where teenagers talk about cutting."

"They make it sound cool," Mia chimes in.

You don't say a lot because, honestly, you're not sure how to respond. You thank the girls for bringing this to your attention, assure them they've done the right thing, and fumble for your phone. As they walk away, you see the time glowing on your screen. It's 10 p.m.

Discussion Questions

As you answer these questions for both scenarios above, think about what would work for your particular school and school community (students, parents, faculty, administration).

1 How do you understand the student's/students' decision to share this information with you?
2 What else would you want to learn if you found yourself in this situation? How might you obtain this information? Are there any barriers to gathering it?
3 What factors might you consider re: how to serve the needs of the student(s)?
4 Are there any "action steps" you will consider? Are there any barriers to taking these steps?
5 Would you consider pulling a colleague into the loop? If so, why and who?

6 Does someone need to contact a parent? If so, why and who?

7 Might there be any barriers to engaging the student (or family)?

8 Is there a role for a school counselor or other mental health professional here?

9 Is there anything in this situation that speaks to an existing school policy, or might inform a new one?

2

The Adolescent Mind

My life started to go downhill in eighth grade …

– tenth grader

Monica, an eighth grader, has always been a strong student. Respected and enjoyed by her teachers, she's one of those over-achieving kids who seems to put a lot of pressure on herself to do her work thoroughly and at a high level. She also seems to have mixed feelings about middle school, primarily for social reasons. While she has had some close friendships, she's suffered more than her share of disappointment and exclusion lately due to some troubling dynamics among groups of girls in her grade.

One morning, Monica's history teacher stops by the dean of students' office to tell the dean that Monica's latest essay contains several sentences that appear to be copied directly from an internet literary analysis source. Since plagiarism violates the school code, it goes beyond being a classroom issue. The teacher wants to know how the school wants her to handle this infraction with Monica.

I presented this scenario to deans of students at a professional development workshop. I then asked them to discuss

DOI: 10.4324/9781003358923-3

how they would counsel the teacher. I was pleased to hear the emphasis of their conversations shift between school policy (was the policy clear, did the student understand what plagiarism was and why it was unacceptable), social-emotional exploration (what might have driven Monica to plagiarize), and disciplinary responses (what the consequences should be and what purpose they should serve).

Drawing on their lived experiences with students, they asked a slew of psychologically-minded questions: What exposure had Monica had to academic integrity policies? What might have motivated her? How and when did this happen? Was there a connection between Monica's social disappointments and her impulse to cut corners on her assignment? What were her reasoning abilities? Where are eighth graders when it comes to moral decision-making?

One dean reasoned:

> If she were in sixth grade, we would view it as a learning opportunity and probably not respond with any penalty. But by eighth grade, I think we can expect *our* kids to understand what we've been telling them every year— you can't copy other people's words without attribution. So maybe there should be consequences in this instance.

To which another added, "But with an eighth grader, we might still view our response to this transgression as a learning opportunity more than a serious violation. Of course, if she were in high school, it would be a different story."

I may have been the only licensed therapist in the room, but these deans were thinking like psychologists. Though they didn't label their frameworks as such, their thoughts and questions revealed developmentally informed considerations of Monica. These deans were actively working to understand this student, to put her plagiarism in the context of her maturity level, and from that knowledge formulate a meaningful and constructive response. No one was looking to merely enforce rules for rules' sake, nor were they inclined to sweep the incident under the rug.

With basic knowledge about psychosocial development and where students are on their developmental trajectory, you are better able to understand how your students think and why they behave as they do. When we understand adolescents' strengths, their limitations, what's going on with them emotionally, and how it all works together to inform their interpretations of the world, our own responses to their behaviors are better informed and more constructive. Moreover, we can anticipate certain behaviors within a given stage and capitalize on that awareness to tailor the content of our curriculum, instruction methods, and classroom management to the benefit of our students, our school communities, and ourselves.

Teenagers Are Not Adults

You, too, probably already think somewhat like a developmental psychologist, whether you know it or not. Maybe you were drawn to secondary education because you're in touch with your "inner teen" and intuitively relate to your students. You understand that adolescents are not miniature versions of adults. You recognize that your students are not simply intellectual learners but are evolving beings grappling every day with who they are and who they might become. And you know from your own experience that the "evolving" part makes them very different from fully mature human beings when it comes to their reasoning abilities, impulse control, emotional lives, and priorities.

While all the above may sound obvious here on the page, these things are often hard to keep in mind during our daily interactions with students. This can be especially true the older our students get. Some high-school students look like adults and from time to time appear to think and talk in sophisticated ways that can lead even an experienced psychologist like myself to forget how young—and therefore how different from us—they are.

We are predisposed to see a given situation through our own perspective, which in our case is an adult one. Compounding our natural bias, the culture of the United States (and many cultures around the world) prioritizes adult perspectives and values. This makes a certain sense; adults create our societies, our institutions (including schools), and the rules that go along with them. And most adults interact primarily with other adults.

For those of us who work with people who are not adults, however, allowing ourselves to default to an adult-centered perspective becomes a block to our effectiveness. It may impede our consideration of our students' perspectives, priorities, and values—meaning we can miss important things. Swayed by this bias, we believe we're being thorough and rational, when maybe we're not fully comprehending a situation. We may think we're doing what's best when our response might be ineffectual or—worse—harmful.

For instance, teenager, who are developmentally driven to compare themselves to their peers, are not reassured tehn we tell them that what other kids think of them doesn't matter—even if in our adult world that seems true. It also isn't effective to use threats of a "ruined future" as a deterrent. Most teens can rarely anticipate anything more than a few months—or sometimes, a few minutes—in the future.

This is such a common hurdle for parents and educators that social scientists have given the phenomenon a name: "adultcentrism." Studies on this subject have found that not only are we unable to broaden our thinking beyond our adult perspective, but our rigid point of view steers us toward invalidating the child's perspective. We do all this without conscious awareness. Like much of bias, adultcentrism mostly happens automatically, so we don't give ourselves a chance to evaluate and perhaps amend our judgments.

As the adults in the room, however, it falls on us to cultivate some awareness of our adult-centric bias. We need to learn to pause our thinking, breathe, and reflect on where students are developmentally—what the situation or interaction looks like from their perspective—before we react.

When you open yourself to engaging with your students, players, or advisees on their level, you have a much better shot at connecting with them in a meaningful way. When kids sense you understand their vantage point and have their interests in mind, they tend to be more accessible and responsive. I cultivate this kind of understanding for myself through asking questions of the student I'm working with. If what they are doing does not make sense to me, I try to discover how it makes sense to *them*, how they understand their own feelings or actions.

This perspective-switching comes more easily to some of us than others. But with awareness and lots of practice, we can all develop it.

Teenagers Are Predictable

Becoming even more familiar with certain aspects of adolescent development can inform our thinking and help us to catch our own bias. It can also assist us in better understanding what our students are going through and the arc of their growth as they progress through middle and high school.

There are some developmental trends you can't help but notice when you've worked in a school for a while. You have likely seen for yourself that adolescents pass through predictable stages of psychosocial as well as biological development. For example, sophomore "summer pop," where many students return to school for their junior year with what seems like a lot more than a summer's worth of physical and sometimes social development on board. And you know from your classroom experience that seventeen-year-olds are very different in dependable ways from their twelve-year-old counterparts. You also know from experience that each of your students is an individual. As we established in the last chapter, while developmental stages are predictable, each adolescent will move through this extended, complex stage at their own pace.

When it comes to defining the developmental stages of adolescence, twentieth-century psychologist Erik Erikson's theory of psychosocial development is probably the best known and most relied on (though it requires updates—more on that later.) His theory identifies eight stages from infancy to old age. Each stage centers on a particular psychological "task" of healthy growth and an inherent conflict that motivates human beings toward mastering that task. The two stages that occur in the middle- and high-school years are labeled "Industry vs. Inferiority" (ages five to twelve) and "Identity vs. Role Confusion" (ages twelve to eighteen). In the former, children are developing a sense of competence at key tasks, the most prominent of which in American culture is academics. In the latter, kids are figuring out not only what they're good at but who they are.

When you understand what a student's stage requires of them and what their motivations are, the student's perspective—the lens through which they view and judge their world and themselves—comes into sharper focus. This knowledge then provides you with cues as to how best to engage them and allows you to be more deliberate in choosing words, actions, and even systems within your classroom that connect with them and help them grow psychosocially, as well as academically.

Industry vs. Inferiority: "Am I Competent?"

At ages eleven and twelve, most sixth and some seventh graders are at the tail end of the "Industry vs. Inferiority" stage. They are teetering on entering adolescence but aren't there yet. So, they have a different perspective and different motivations from most of their eighth- and ninth-grade schoolmates—and from you, their teacher.

According to Erikson, the tension in this stage is between developing a sense of personal competency or of inadequacy/failure. Since they entered kindergarten and the world beyond their family, students have been hard at work expanding their capabilities both academically and socially. Learning to read. Manipulating numbers. Making friends. Riding a bike. Playing on a team. These skills they've built over the last six years have also built their self-esteem—or threatened or diminished it.

During this stage, students in American schools have moved from learning for learning's sake—and being for "being's sake"—to being evaluated and judged on their academic skills and on who they are within their social circles. By the time they reach sixth grade, most kids have become masters at comparing themselves to others to get a handle on how and whether they measure up.

When this stage progresses smoothly, students achieve confidence in their abilities and in themselves. They are unafraid to challenge themselves and explore their worlds, with one success paving the way for others.

When it doesn't go so well, the student may develop a sense of "inferiority" and a fear of failure. This can limit their willingness to try new things and make them reluctant to ask for help. I've seen this in numerous students with undiagnosed or inadequately managed learning disabilities. When an adolescent attempts to function without a clear understanding of what's getting in the way of their progress, let alone a map for how to make progress or shift course, they struggle not just with schoolwork but with psychosocial development.

Throughout this stage, children look to both their parents and teachers for approval, support, and affirmation of their growing competencies. Certainly, by eleven or twelve years old, a student's gaze is starting to shift toward their peer group for approval. Still, the adults in their life continue to feature prominently in their self-evaluation and need for affirmation. It's hard to overestimate how what you think of them and how it's conveyed matters and shapes what they think of themselves.

When engaging students in this stage of development, it's essential to encourage and acknowledge their achievements, and crucial to attend to any stumbling blocks. We never want students to feel incompetent or inadequate.

At the same time, we don't want to protect students from their own mistakes or vulnerabilities, especially when we or other adults can readily help. We want to teach students to view challenges or problems as having remedies that will allow future success and to deal with them in a healthy way. Sometimes this means individualizing an assignment to accommodate varied learning styles (e.g., verbal vs. visual presentation of material) or levels. Other times, it means showing your weakest math student that you're excited about and respectful of what a good football player they are (i.e., even if they aren't great at math, they're still a valuable person in your eyes).

As an adult to whom your students are looking to evaluate themselves, you can participate in this stage of their development by helping them to make competence and self-worth part of their foundation, whatever the details.

Identity vs. Role Confusion: "Who Am I?"

From approximately ages twelve to eighteen, according to Erikson, your students developmentally are focused on defining who they are as they inch ever closer to full adulthood. The tension in this stage is between achieving a sense of self or entering adulthood confused as to who they are and what they value. As we all know from our own adolescence, this search for identity tends to involve quite a bit of trial and error.

When this stage goes well, a young adult emerges with fidelity to their self-crafted identity. They can align their actions and decisions to their newly defined core values as they take on more and more responsibility for themselves.

When adolescents are unable to embrace an identity, they enter adulthood as unsure and possibly insecure individuals. They don't know what they value or their own mind, making them vulnerable to less optimal—even self-destructive—choices in their adult life.

In an effort to define themselves as individuals, adolescents often first push against the expectations and values that their parents and culture have set out for them. While today's students are more familiar and emotionally closer to their parents than previous generations, they are nonetheless on a quest to separate psychologically and claim their own place in the world. Some students might still embrace their parents' values and identities, wishing to follow in their footsteps. However, others will consider and pursue identities in direct opposition to those of their parents. This pulling away is a very natural part of growing up.

As they push their parents out, many students, as we've already learned, continue to seek adult input. So, they turn to teachers, a more acceptable adult resource during this developmental period. But make no mistake, peers are the most important relational focus for students in the middle- and secondary-school years. Paradoxically, as adolescents seek to individuate, they want nothing more than to fit in with their friends. During this period, adolescents are hard-wired to care deeply about what their peers think of them and to rely on peers for emotional support.

Due to both ignorance of consequences and urgency to belong, students are likely to make some unwise choices about what they are willing to do to be part of the group. Risky behaviors increase due to this strong drive for connection, inclusion, and approval—a.k.a. peer pressure. Note that peer pressure is not limited to friends literally coaxing or cajoling each other to try or do risky or ill-advised things. It can be much more subtle and derive from a teenager's own internal need to emulate certain admired peers or integrate into a group.

Interestingly, this adolescent propensity for risk is a trait that can be found across species. Research has shown that mice imbibe more alcohol when hanging out with their mice peers than when they are alone. While the image of drunk mice at an off-campus party might seem far-fetched, this type of animal research validates the argument that a lot of adolescent behavior seems, like so much else in this stage of development, biologically driven. (More on risk-taking in Chapter 3.)

When it comes to establishing friendships and deciding whom to trust, the lessons learned throughout this stage—both good and bad—build the scaffolding and support necessary to foster authentic, healthy relationships throughout life. The intensity of adolescent friendships lays the groundwork for later years or stages.

Your students' developmentally appropriate drive to push against cultural norms may make them provocative. Throughout their middle- and high-school years, they're going to try on different belief systems, dress and hair styles, and social roles—all in pursuit of reconciling who they have been and who they might become. They may say and do things that from our adult perspective are not well thought out or prudent. Through all of this, our students are generally testing the boundaries to see what new things feels like.

If you were this sort of teenager, you may "get it." Or you may be so chagrined by your own misadventures that you've blocked any empathy you might have for similar souls. If you were a cautious, rule-abiding adolescent, as a subset of teachers undoubtedly were, find a respected adult in your midst who wasn't and ask them to share their perspective and adolescent experience with you.

Development Isn't Linear

Erikson's model of psychosocial development, conceived in the middle of the twentieth century, can be enhanced by systems updates. For instance, human beings don't necessarily follow Erikson's stages in a discrete, linear fashion—and we need to keep that in mind as we engage with individual students.

Sometimes a person moves to a new stage before completing the previous one. The notion of "complete" developmental stages is not nearly as important or accepted by more contemporary psychologists. All we need to do is look in the mirror to know that identity development does not "end" or "resolve" by the time we graduate from high school or college.

Still, the notion that adolescence is a time of intense identity formation rings true from our own lived experiences and from observing students. What we can use from Erikson's model is the notion that, with each passing year from middle school through high school, in general our students' priorities are shifting from building competencies to an all-out emphasis on identity. This allows us to grasp the tenets of developmental psychology, so what students do, how they act and react, make much more sense.

For instance, Erikson's theory of development provides us with practical insight into why a middle-school student, who was so focused on academics, athletics, and music in elementary school, now only seems to care about what to wear and where they're going to sit at lunch. Where once we might have labeled that student as "distracted," we now know that developmentally speaking they're not distracted at all. They're doing the important and necessary work of maturing. Rather than straying from the path, they're right on course.

We also know it's up to us to shift our perspective and meet students where they are. One unusual and compelling strategy for developing a greater understanding of our students comes from Phyllis Fagel, school counselor at Sheridan School in Washington, D.C., and author of the 2018 book, *Middle School Matters: The 10 Key Skills Kids Need to Thrive in Middle School and Beyond, and How Parents Can Help*. In her blog post titled, *5 Ways Teachers Can Bring Out the Best in Middle School Students*, she relays that at her middle school, every staff member is required to shadow a student for an entire day. The purpose is to gain insight into and empathy for challenges students face that we adults may be unaware of, as well as how students process those challenges developmentally.

I recommend this exercise for high-school teachers as well. It's easy to lose sight of what our students are up against hour to hour. Walking a few steps in their shoes would, of course, enhance your understanding. If you find this directive highly impractical, simply note its spirit. Try asking your students about their experiences and perspectives while demonstrating your willingness to listen.

We must keep in mind that tackling these complex developmental tasks requires energy and attention. So, students' inability to concentrate in algebra class—while neither a productive nor sustainable modus operandi—becomes more understandable, even expected at times. With this understanding and expectation, our minds can open to working on ways to reach our students on a personal level, so as to ensure academic learning occurs alongside psychosocial growth.

For example, instead of growling, "Sophie, pay attention!" as you are inclined to do on your worst days, you might instead consider gesturing to Sophie after class or shooting her a note to say something like, "You looked like maybe you were having trouble paying attention in class today. Is there anything I can do to help?" If something is troubling her, Sophie may appreciate that you noticed her. She may even take you up on your offer of help with math or something entirely separate. And even if Sophie was simply distracted and bored, your concern might remind her that you are teaching for her personal benefit, and it matters to you that she makes an effort to follow along.

Sexuality, Gender, and Racial Identity

Another limitation of Erikson's theory—like many Western psychological theories of the 1950s—is that it's male-centered and does not account for differences in social or cultural context.

Today, psychologists of adolescence are keenly focused on racial identity and a full spectrum of sexual and gender identity. Both are areas that many teenagers are extremely aware of within themselves, as individuals and as group members. To appreciate the factors and pressures shaping our students' perspectives, attitudes, and behaviors, we must also better understand these facets of the self.

As all of us in education are aware, most Gen Z-ers are more knowledgeable and much less reticent in talking about racial, sexual, and gender identity than previous generations. They confront these subjects with openness and honesty. Developmentally speaking, it's important for us educators to be aware that these identity factors are coming into play for middle- and high-school students in a way they didn't earlier in their lives. (We'll take a take a deeper dive into key features of race and ethnicity, gender identity, and sexual orientation, as well as social class, in Section II of this book.)

Somewhere between early adolescence and emerging adulthood (college and one's twenties) most students become aware of the potential for romantic relationships. Consequently, their search for sexual identity gains a sense of urgency. Unlike in past generations, the fluidity of that identity is increasingly acceptable today. While this is a positive development, it also presents more choices about self-definition, which means more for adolescents to sort through and figure out.

When it comes to racial identity, psychologists know that teenagers of color—for example, Black teenagers in the United States—place more emphasis on their racial identity than white students. In her 1997 (updated in 2017) book, *Why Are All the Black Kids Sitting Together in the Cafeteria?*, clinical psychologist and president emerita of Spelman College, Beverly Tatum, informs her readers that it's more common to see racially mixed groups of elementary school children playing and sitting together than it is to see integrated groups of older students in racially mixed school environments. She further explains that Black students stay close together in middle school and high school because being Black has become salient in their developmentally predictable quest for identity. She writes:

> Why do Black youths, in particular, think about themselves in terms of race? Because that is how the world thinks of them. Our perceptions are shaped by the messages that we receive from those around us, and when young Black men and women enter adolescence, the racial content of those messages intensifies.

Twenty-five years after their initial publication, the examples and contexts in Tatum's book remain strikingly relevant.

Today's Normal Is Not All That Normal

Adolescence is complicated, confusing, and messy in the best of circumstances. Unfortunately, Gen Z is not living in the best of circumstances. Systemic threats to our society and our world—such as school gun violence, tremendous family income disparities, social issues of racial and gender discrimination, climate change, and polarized politics, not to mention a global pandemic—intersect and interact with this tenuous time in their development.

Many of today's students are actively thinking about bigger issues than themselves, in large part because they have so much more access to information than any previous generation. They've never known a world without iPhones, Facebook, Instagram, or TikTok. Even if they want to tune out bigger issues, it's harder than ever to do so. And many Gen Z students are affected by the larger issues (racial injustice, economic inequity, sexual harassment, homophobia) in deeply personal ways, sometimes on a daily basis.

Living with these threats and uncertainties beyond the individual's control—results in constant, simmering stress just beneath the surface of students' consciousness. These pressures and threats strain family dynamics as well. For example, we know that when parents and caregivers struggle, their children can be deeply affected. These larger factors undoubtedly contribute to increased rates of anxiety, depression, self-injurious behavior, and suicidal thoughts and behaviors among middle- and high-school students.

Ten years ago, the middle- and high-school students I saw in my practice talked primarily about themselves, as expected. Gen Z-ers are the first students I've had who regularly discuss broad public issues like global warming during their individual sessions.

Along with all the normal developmental challenges of adolescence, today's students have the weight of the world on their minds—minds that aren't yet fully formed. I hear from teachers and administrators all over the country about the dramatic increase in student mental health needs in their schools. Schools that have the resources are increasing counseling, academic/ learning support, and other services. Many of them can't hire fast enough.

All this must be considered as we interact with this generation and do all we can to encourage their academic, emotional, and social development.

Burgeoning Capacities

As students move through the arc of each developmental stage, capacities that will bloom fully in the next stage are beginning to take shape and make appearances from time to time. It's well worth your effort (and even kind of fun) to look out for and encourage these burgeoning psychological capacities—self-awareness, self-management, and moral judgement—in your students.

The act of trying on new identities in and of itself sets the stage for self-awareness to emerge. This process requires that teenagers look closely at themselves, judge themselves, figure out what they value, and ask again and again if their behavior aligns with these values. This is why—as you've likely observed— high school seniors, on the whole, are markedly more self-aware than eighth graders.

In time, the combination of this emerging self-awareness and the continuing development of their brain's prefrontal cortex enables each high schooler to (sporadically) link behaviors and outcomes, laying the groundwork for more effective self-management. On occasion, they start to think before they act or speak. Risky behaviors diminish somewhat as students age. When development proceeds successfully, they show signs of taking more responsibility for themselves. They begin to understand that there are consequences for actions and that even in the face of perceived or very real unfairness, they have some agency and choice in how they handle the events in their lives.

Finally, as their thinking and reasoning skills evolve, adolescents' moral awareness develops as well. If you've ever played a board game with a five- or six-year-old, you may have noticed they're not always the most honest or ethical participants. Cheating is rampant at this age because children are only just beginning to understand that it's wrong to break the rules by taking an extra turn, grabbing unearned bonuses, or even turning the board upside down in response to losing. So, while it may not be all that much fun to play games with them, you probably don't worry about their mental health.

If a twelve-year-old cheats, it's a lot more concerning. We expect older kids to "know better." If a sixteen- or seventeen-year-old cheats at a game, you might even feel the need to take them aside and ask what's going on. That's because in adolescence, kids are developing the capacity for more sophisticated, abstract reasoning, which paves the way for nuanced moral reasoning. I emphasize "developing" because this is, like everything else at this age, a work in progress.

I've seen some educators (and parents) make the mistaken assumption that their middle- or high-school student's level of moral reasoning and ethical behavior is fixed, a feature of their personality. It's not. These aspects of our minds and characters continue developing well into adulthood. A college student who cheats on an exam in a moment of panic won't necessarily be prone to cheat on their tax returns or submit false overtime claims at age thirty.

Limited or faulty moral reasoning is typically outgrown through maturation and life experience. While we can't predict the future in any single case, I tend to refrain from doing so even when I think I can, especially if my prediction is pessimistic.

As a psychologist who keeps in touch with students over extended periods of time (sometimes decades), I've seen growth and change into adulthood that I wouldn't have expected or even dreamed of. The failing high-school student who became a prominent author. The disaffected teenager who became a gifted teacher. The drug-abusing adolescent who became an award-winning chef. The disempowered kid from an under-resourced school who was elected to city council. All of them found themselves not only through therapy but also through relationships with teachers and mentors who believed in them, even when a lot of other people didn't. If you happen to have been one of these kids yourself, you can probably identify a trusted adult who made a big difference. Maybe they are even a reason you went into education.

As middle- and secondary-school educators, one of our aims should be and can be to encourage our students' growing moral capacities. Richard Weissbourd, director of Harvard University's Making Caring Common Project, argues that schools can play a larger role in helping students develop empathy and caring for others, alongside fostering achievement and happiness.

To encourage such effort, the project's Caring Community Youth Capstone Program provides strategies for integrating "habits of caring and ethical reflection" into the classroom curriculum and school community. This is a semester- or year-long experience that engages eighth through twelfth graders in a series of meetings and projects designed to build empathy, ethical awareness, and caring. Examples listed in the downloadable "how-to guide" (https://mcc.gse.harvard.edu/resources-for-educators/caring-community-youth-capstone-strategy) include writing a biography of a community member who has been "invisible" and developing a video game that promotes perspective-taking and a sense of responsibility for others.

Even if you don't have the bandwidth to engage in the full, large-scale project with your students, you might pick and choose ideas from the project and its guide to incorporate into your class or advisory.

Programs like Making Caring Common remind us that adolescents are cognitively and emotionally capable of developing ethical identities in which they care for others. But as with learning grammar or algebra, they benefit from scaffolding that shapes and shepherds their development.

The Gift of the Adolescent Mind

Because of where they are along the psychosocial growth continuum, tweens and teens do us a service: They keep us honest. They demand transparency. They are quick to perceive and point out inconsistencies and contradictions—a reflection of their increasing cognitive capacities for reason and logic, as well as their striving toward independent thinking and decision-making. They ask the questions we as adults may have long ago settled or rationalized away in our own minds.

The students I've come to know model, challenge, and inspire. They keep me in touch with aspects of my younger self that otherwise would have faded beyond recognition. They were welcome companions for me on Zoom calls during the height of the COVID-19 pandemic closures and isolation. They welcomed me into their homes (noisy or quiet, large or small, messy or neat). Their backdrops inevitably showcased their signature posters, string lights, artwork, and photographs. I hear from teachers across the country and across grade levels that despite the extreme strain of professional life in the 2020s, their students remain the most beautiful, brightest lights in their midst.

It's a major responsibility to educate an evolving adolescent mind. It is also a gift to witness their development, to be there to support and guide them as they transition from childhood to nascent adulthood.

Talk It Out: A Scenario and Questions for Discussion

Just as you did in Chapter 1, read through the scenario below. Then answer the questions that follow by yourself or with a group of colleagues.

Maggie, an eighth grader, is one of your favorite students. She's always been a leader, both academically and socially. She's serious about learning but always ready to have fun.

For the past two years, Maggie has been part of a small, tight friend group consisting of four other girls in her class. When students return in the fall, it's quite visible that over the summer three of the girls in Maggie's friend group have hit puberty. Their bodies are more developed and their "air" more adolescent. Maggie and another girl, however, look essentially the same as they did in seventh grade.

By winter, you notice that Maggie is uncharacteristically on the fringes of her friend group in the hallways and during lunch. She suddenly seems less central and integrated, and once or twice you think you notice a forlorn look on her face.

One afternoon while you and Maggie are meeting about an upcoming essay assignment, you ask how things are going for her. A sad look flashes across her face, and she says, "Okay ... I mean, things have been better." You wait a minute to give her room to elaborate, and she does. "It's just—I feel like no one likes me anymore. Like we used to have all the exact same interests. Sadie—my best friend—and I were pretty much the same person. Now I just don't know."

Discussion Questions

1 What do you believe is going on with Maggie? What developmental factors might be driving Maggie's emotions?
2 What do you think the situation looks like from Maggie's perspective? And how might this inform your response?
3 What else would you want to know from Maggie? What are your concerns?
4 Is there anything specific you want to ask Maggie? Or tell her?
5 Are there any "action items" to consider?

Bibliography

1) Logue, Sheree, Chein, Jason, Gould, Thomas, Holliday, Erica, and Steinberg, Laurence. (2014) Adolescent mice, unlike adults, consume more alcohol in the presence of peers than alone. *Developmental Science* 17(1): 79–85.
2) Fagel, Phyllis. (2018) *Middle School Matters: The 10 Key Skills Kids Need to Thrive in Middle School and Beyond, and How Parents Can Help.* Hachette Book.
3) Fagel, Phyllis. (2020) *5 Ways Teachers Can Bring Out the Best in Middle School Students.* Association for Supervision and Curriculum Development (ASCD), published on January 1, 2020.
4) Tatum, Beverly. (1997; Updated 2017) *Why Are All the Black Kids Sitting Together in the Cafeteria?* Basic Books.
5) Weissbourd, Richard. Faculty Director: Making Caring Common. https://mcc.gse.harvard.edu/; https://mcc.gse.harvard.edu/resources-for-educators/caring-community-youth-capstone-strategy

3

They Did What? Risk, Reward, and Impulsivity

> Looking back on some of my teenage mistakes is humbling … at best.
>
> – School Counselor

So now we have a sense of where our students are developmentally, and we understand some of the thought processes and psychological motivations behind their behaviors. But just because "typical" teen behaviors are less of a mystery to us doesn't make the most infamous of them—impulsivity and risk-taking—any less disruptive in their lives … or ours. Taken together (impulsivity and risk-taking frequently manifest as a package deal), these "very natural," "totally understandable," "developmentally appropriate" adolescent inclinations can interfere with your instruction, your coaching, and sometimes the workings of the entire school community.

There's no need to surrender to biology on this front. If appreciated, anticipated, and given direction, these adolescent drives can be tapped and used productively—and in ways that encour-

DOI: 10.4324/9781003358923-4

age those burgeoning capacities and give students experience in managing themselves in more thoughtful, independent ways. For instance, the same developmental itch that makes teens want generate chaos can be directed into making meaningful challenges to the status quo, with the added incentive of affecting positive change.

"How Am I Supposed to Think About Consequences Before They Happen?"

Helping adolescents to manage their risk-taking begins with understanding that you are up against two major developmental fronts: a tendency toward impulsivity in general and a penchant for reward-seeking (the catalyst for much impulsive risk-taking).

Most psychologists and neuroscientists have agreed for a long time that adolescent brain development is multifaceted and uneven. The subcortical structures ("reward-seeking" regions or "pleasure centers") of the brain mature earlier than the cerebral cortex (the decision-making center), which processes thoughts and assesses risk. So, there's a biological or anatomical underpinning to students' tendency to seek reward while minimizing or discounting risk. This has been the conventional wisdom, and it's not wrong.

Laurence Steinberg, an expert on adolescent psychology, proposes a "dual systems" model of adolescent risk-taking (also known as the maturation imbalance theory). He based this on his study of approximately 1,000 socioeconomically and racially diverse individuals between the ages of ten and thirty. He found that "reward-seeking" increased between preadolescence and mid-adolescence, and then subsequently declined. Interestingly, Steinberg's study also demonstrated that starting at around age ten, impulsivity is in actuality on the wane. Thus—Steinberg argues—the propensity for risk-taking or ill-advised behavior in middle adolescence (from about eighth to eleventh grade) "may be due to the combination of relatively higher inclinations to seek rewards and still maturing capacities for self-control." (Steinberg, Laurence. 2010. A dual systems model of adolescent risk-taking. *Developmental Psychobiology* 52(3): 216–224.)

While it's true that adolescents can be hardy and resilient in the face of stressors and problems, their relative imbalance in brain function also makes them biologically and psychologically more vulnerable to making poorly informed choices than the average adult. They react to situations without much consideration of outcomes or consequences, while at the same time discounting risk and rarely entertaining a second thought. As these obstacles to level-headedness present themselves, their more fully developed "pleasure centers" are pumping out dopamine, making the adolescent more susceptible to saying "yes" to behaviors that look irrational at best and, at worst, self-destructive.

Needless to say, this is why youth marketing is such a high intensity, high expenditure strategy for commercial advertisers. Teenagers are easy marks when it comes to product purchases, whether sneakers, energy drinks, or vapes. They want what they want when they want it and tend to grab it (no matter the price) with abandon.

Risk-taking Isn't All Bad

Saying "yes" to new experiences without thinking isn't always a negative, however. In fact, a teenager's willingness to dive headlong into the unknown with enthusiasm is essential to their development. Their reward-seeking, impulsivity, and discounting of risk don't just cause them to drive too fast or FaceTime until 3 a.m. on a school night, these impulses also give adolescents the initiative and the nerve to explore, experiment, and challenge—sometimes everything and everyone. And these experiences are the very things that enable them to learn and mature.

Through experience—good and bad—an adolescent's capacity for impulse control naturally evolves and a more discerning person often emerges. Phrases like "That might not be the best idea," "If I don't turn this paper in on time, I'll lose ten points off the top," or "But how would we get home?" begin to show up from time to time in their decision-making. In other words, they steadily—though still not reliably—mature.

If you've taught across grade levels, you've likely witnessed evidence of this process. You've seen in real time those ninth graders whose crumpled homework routinely disappeared in their backpacks transform into seniors who are now relatively organized and on top of their game. In fact, when students don't progress developmentally, you may intuitively step back and wonder what's getting in their way.

Not All Risks Are Created Equal

Many of the lessons learned during this period of growth, however, are hard ones. Some are sadly irreversible. And even after negative experiences, some kids continue to pursue the "reward" despite the costs.

Neuroscientist Adrienne Romer and her colleagues Valerie Reyna and Seth Pardo wondered if it were possible to predict which teenagers would express their risk-taking tendencies in adaptive and helpful ways and which would tend more toward dangerous and maladaptive risk-taking. So, they conducted a longitudinal study that divided reward-seeking into two categories: 1) reward sensitivity—the desire to seek novel experiences, to set and reach goals, to achieve something—and 2) sensation seeking—the desire to feel something, like a thrill or a high.

After surveying approximately 1,000 subjects, they found those who were more reward sensitive were also more likely to take adaptive risks—such as joining a protest for a cause they believed in, studying abroad for a semester, or speaking in public. Meanwhile, subjects who fell more into the sensation-seeking category were more likely to take maladaptive risks—such as having regrettable or even dangerous sex, sneaking out, or experimenting with alcohol and drugs. (The study did find that some of the more reward-sensitive subjects did engage in underage drinking but suggested the behavior was motivated by a desire to belong, rather than a drive to become intoxicated.)

"Rash impulsive" action (acting without thinking) and the discounting of potential risk were exclusive to sensation seeking and maladaptive risk behaviors. Worth noting, male subjects were much more likely to take risks than female subjects.

Some of the adolescent sensation seekers in Romer's study did go on to develop problem behaviors. However, one piece of reassuring news is that the majority of subjects appeared to learn from their experiences. Even within the sensation-seeking group, most did not develop long-term problem behaviors. (Romer et al., 2016.)

The Risk-taking Spectrum

Though Romer's study placed reward-seekers into relatively discrete categories (in part because that's how research works best), you may have observed for yourself that impulsivity and risk-taking don't always present themselves this way in real life. Individual adolescents don't necessarily fall into just one category a hundred percent of the time. Impulsivity and risk-taking can pop up from time to time even in generally thoughtful, cautious, super "sane" kids. Across any group of adolescents, these tendencies also fall along a broad continuum.

At one end of this spectrum is behavior that is oppositional to the point of defiance. These are the kids who consistently and seemingly willfully break the rules (and sometimes even the law), eventually causing serious harm to themselves and sometimes their communities. Their behavior is extreme and pathological. Fortunately, it's also a psychological and statistical outlier.

On the other end of the spectrum is strict rule-following behavior—a refusal to take a risk, to question where the lines are drawn, let alone color outside them. While rule-adherence might not present a threat to the school community at large—and is likely even welcomed and praised by adults—it can be detrimental to a teen's development.

As we alluded to in the last chapter, adolescents who "skip over" any assertions of autonomy (like rebellion and risk-taking) miss important pieces of the normative developmental journey. So, students who always defer to outside authority to define their values and determine their behavior may miss out on developing a strong, independent sense of self—and ultimately struggle in some ways. Not only does excessive adherence to rules and regulations not go over well with adolescent peers, it also deprives an adolescent of the mastery experiences that come from pushing the limits from time to time.

Middle-spectrum Thinking

Thankfully, most of our students fall comfortably in the middle of this spectrum. This is not to say middle-of-the-road adolescents can't find their way into destructive or dangerous moves. Perfectly "normal" teenagers occasionally make potentially life-harming decisions, such as shoplifting, abusing alcohol and drugs, engaging in risky sex or coercing sexual behavior from others, or putting themselves or others in danger through reckless driving or physical fights. In their minds, these behaviors seem worth the risk at a given moment—in part because they can't fathom what or how serious the actual consequences could be. When natural consequences inevitably arrive, they can come as a shock.

But on most days with most students, unwise behaviors show up in more mundane ways and lean more toward the disruptive than the dangerous. For instance, some middle- or high-school students consistently fail to complete assignments, are reliably late to class, challenge everything we say, are unable to sustain attention through a class period, and sometimes can't seem to follow the simplest directions. Most vexing, when "called out" on these behaviors, some of these kids respond with flimsy or unrealistic excuses.

When I was a school counselor, I absorbed teachers' frustration and dismay as they told me of yet another student's insistence that their assignment had been submitted on time and was at that very moment sitting in the teacher's front-office mailbox or Google Drive folder. In these cases, it would inevitably turn out, of course, that the assignment was not in any such place. It was squarely residing in the student's imagination.

When I would later confront these students and ask why they would tell a lie that was sure to reveal itself sooner rather than later, student after student would confide that it was easier to avoid the discomfort and embarrassment in the moment than to consider the possibility that if (or when) the truth came out things would surely go from bad to worse. It routinely caught me—an adult—by surprise that, to them, their choice felt entirely rational (at the time, anyway).

Call it wishful thinking, misrepresentation, or—yes—lying, but fabricating a story that's bound to unravel is another one of those typical adolescent risk-taking, reward-seeking behaviors. Part of what's going on here is that the adolescent mind is so powerful and their imaginations so active that they can more easily slip into magical thinking than an adult can. They think if they intended to do the assignments—and what's more, really wish they had done it—it's as good as complete. And as a psychologist, I find it useful never to underestimate the power of denial.

As we've discussed, most adolescents live in the moment and adhere to the "pleasure principle" in which pleasure is consistently sought and pain avoided if at all possible. Short-term comfort and gain are generally preferable to—well—anything else. This tendency, along with their inability to anticipate or appreciate long-term outcomes, which we've established they come by honestly, make adolescents susceptible to behaviors that may drive the adults in their life a little crazy.

Though it seems unbelievable through our "adult-centric" lenses, the students described above are unable to come to grips with the fact their excuses won't hold up and they are sure to be "found out"—a wholly predictable negative outcome most adults would see as inevitable.

All this comes into bright focus when working with students who have engaged in a more serious violation of academic integrity. Remember Monica, the eighth grader at the start of Chapter 2, who plagiarized? Students who I've worked with in similar predicaments have explained to me that, in a panic the night before an assignment is due, they "reasoned" that copying language from someone else's work was a smarter choice than owning up to the truth of their procrastination, writing what they could, and getting a bad grade. That's the extent of their problem-solving capabilities.

Most have no comprehension of the harm of plagiarism or the high probability that they'll be caught and that the consequences will be worse than a bad grade. Those things simply don't factor into their problem-solving or decision-making. And to be fair, Gen Z-ers consume so much content from universally accessible "open access" electronic sources—from Wikipedia to TikTok—it's hard for them to appreciate the legal, ethical, or spiritual aspects of intellectual property.

If we are being honest with ourselves … as adults, we still find ourselves inclined in moments to cover up the truth to get out of a jam—often it's our first instinct. We'll drive well over the speed limit to get somewhere important. Or maybe take a micro-snooze during a boring meeting. The difference is we can usually activate our minds to calculate the true "risk" of these actions and then rustle up the good sense and motivation to pull back when necessary. Our students simply lack the ability to do this yet, at least consistently. Their chances of learning how to do it increase dramatically with the scaffolding, support, and guidance that schools and educators provide.

It's also important for us to recognize that adolescents aren't the only ones to misrepresent their work or fail to consider the long-term consequences of misleading people. All we have to do is scan newspaper headlines to see a sizable subset of adults behaving in these ways. The difference developmentally and psychologically is that most students who engage in deception (and self-deception) are in the process of learning to overcome these tendencies. They can—and most will—quite literally "grow out" of them and the impulsiveness that seeds them. It's up to us, as educators, to help them get there.

All this being said, it's probably time for a disclaimer here: Just as I see adolescents acting in developmentally appropriate but potentially precarious ways, I also routinely observe them doing courageous, kind, and admirable things. All the time. I expect you do, too.

Facing Reality and Using It for Good

As I write this, schools across the country are recovering from the fall 2021 scourge known as "TikTok Challenges." As a middle- or high-school teacher, I'm sure you are all too aware that TikTok is a video-sharing app that allows users to create and share videos on any topic. It has captivated the teenage market.

Like all social media platforms, TikTok can be used for good—self-expression, peer education, building community—or for more malevolent aims. The "TikTok Challenge" videos unfortunately fall into the latter. They encouraged and inspired acts of vandalism and violence. One documented a student tearing soap dispensers from a bathroom wall. Another, which circulated under the tagline "devious licks," showed a student slapping a teacher.

Overnight, these videos became ubiquitous, riveting adolescents along with adults to their devastating images. These images proved irresistible to adolescent minds. They were at once outrageous, rebellious, risky, and sensational—not to mention dazzling with far-ranging social influence. Parents, community leaders, and school systems railed against the TikTok Challenge, wishing they could ban it and looking to extinguish its influence as quickly as possible.

But when the Broward County Public Schools in Florida suffered a rash of student vandalism inspired by "TikTok Challenges," their then superintendent Vickie Cartwright came up with a clever response. She leaned into the students' natural inclination to embrace "challenge" and channeled it toward a more adaptive outcome—social justice. Cartwright dared her system's middle- and high-school students to turn the craze into a force for good. She challenged them—and empowered them—to create TikToks that promoted changes they'd like to see in their schools and in the world.

Cartwright's students took her dare and ran with it. One group sponsored Monday morning pep rallies to bolster school pride. One created and displayed art projects with themes such as kindness and peace. Every participating school made a video of their effort and posted it as part of the great TikTok Challenge with the hashtag #SchoolPrideAndPeace.

Whether or not Cartwright was aware of it, Romer's study on adaptive and maladaptive risk-taking supported this strategy. It had shown that both types of reward-seeking set off dopaminergic pathways (i.e., gave subjects a rush), so adaptive risks can feel just as good as maladaptive ones.

Thus, the students' adolescent brains still got the rewards they're driven to seek—a sense of engagement, autonomy, and competence, with a shot of dopamine. And by earning that reward through generating positive novel experiences and taking productive risks, their brains reinforced the connections toward regular, considered thought and a mature action.

Encouragement Not Judgment. Incentives Not Punishment.

For educators of tweens and teens, there is a lovely lesson here. We can stop trying to squash our students' natural tendencies and instead help them turn them into a "force for good."

What adolescents need from the adults in their lives is encouragement, not judgment. Judgment and punishment tend to make kids feel angry and defeated, as well as giving them yet another thing to reject or push against. It's not helpful or useful to yank adolescents back inside boundaries we construct for them and tell them to stay put, not to mention none of us wants to spend our careers threatening our students into learning. And we certainly don't want to squash their desire to explore, experiment, and—yes—seek sensation. All of those can be good, healthy tendencies when it comes to learning and growth.

Our job now is to foster autonomy—to get our students to make the move from reliance on external regulation to their growing capacity for internal/self-regulation. Teaching is about content, but it's also about process. There's an experiential component to your classes—or team practices or club meetings—that's about your relationship with your students and their relationships with each other. The ways you engage and respond as an educator matter.

You're positioned to provide students with occasions to think, act, and take responsibility for themselves. Take, for instance, the oft-dreaded group project. Many students gripe about them, usually because the organizational structure of group projects tends toward chaos and the workload toward unequal distribution. Still, they are a concrete illustration of how much students can learn in a class that has little to do with the particular subject matter. Whether you are teaching geometry, literature, foreign language, or biology, you can structure your classroom time to provide students opportunities to examine the broader conse-quences of their behaviors. And remember, they also need plenty of room to make mistakes and to reconsider when necessary.

The following are a few classroom management techniques that take advantage of the natural proclivities of the teenage brain for reward-seeking, impulsiveness, and risk-taking, and put them to work in adaptive ways that serve the student (and the classroom environment). Each in its own way aims to take the onus for their behaviors from you and put it on them to learn to manage—under your guidance and watchful eye, of course.

Set Clear Expectations and Boundaries

At the beginning of each semester or grading period, make sure students understand what the expectations are—their responsi-bilities to the class and you, as well as yours to them. Tell them what they can expect to learn and what they can expect from you. Lay out the class policies. Lay out the syllabus and calendar. Explain how they will be graded. Tell them how and when to reach out for help, if needed (and not at the last minute).

I've seen teachers write expectations out as a contract between teacher and student, use a class period to go through each item and answer any questions, and then have the students sign. This way, when magical thinking and outlandish excuses rear their heads, you can use these contracts to bring students back to rational thought and move them toward taking responsi-bility for themselves.

Solicit and Use Student Input

Students should realize that this is their education, their life. Ask for student input at every opportunity. Demonstrate that you're open to their perspective. If they suggest something good, work with them to implement it. If they suggest something outra-geous, don't immediately tell them why they're wrong. Talk it through—person to person—until they reach a more sensible conclusion using their own reasoning. You will get more buy-in from your students about expectations and responsibilities if you give them a voice and respond thoughtfully.

Don't be surprised if a student hesitates or even recedes when you first ask for their opinion. They might need to see if your invitation is "for real" before they settle down. If they continue to be restless or inattentive, use it as an opportunity to ask why. Sometimes (perhaps often) there are issues swirling around the student sector that we haven't yet heard about—a classmate in crisis or an imminent due date for an overwhelming assignment in another class. If there is something about your class that's creating collective unrest, it's important for students to feel comfortable sharing their concerns.

Be Organized

Organization is not the strong suit of many middle- or high-school students. Instead of expecting behaviors they don't yet developmentally have the skills to deliver, model this skill for them and set your class up so it's hard for them not to be organized.

Start with being structured yourself in the way you present material and make assignments. Give your students deadlines, as well as step-by-step procedures for organizing their work and getting it in on time. For instance, when assigning a long-term project or paper, break it down into smaller parts and a series of deadlines for students, keeping them on task and preventing procrastination.

Give them every opportunity to be organized and feel the pleasure of it. Then, be sure to praise them for the behavior. As their skills build, loosen the classroom structure to let them take more responsibility for organizing themselves.

Consider the Limits of the Adolescent Attention Span

When planning lessons and projects take into account the adolescent attention span. Reminder: It's short. So do everything you can to actively engage them.

Experiential education—learning through doing—is always best. When possible, make them responsible to their peers. For instance, allow them to research and present on a special topic of interest to them. Or have students conduct discussion groups. If you must lecture, make it a multimedia presentation. (And if you don't know how to create one, ask your students to teach you—they'll enjoy the role reversal.)

Play to Their Natural Curiosity about the World

If a student asks, "When am I ever going to use (fill in the blank)?" give them a thoughtful, comprehensive answer and invite them to think with you about the application of whatever the subject is in everyday life. Better yet, plan your lessons from day one so that the practical applications of everything from algebra to ancient history are evident. Everything is more interesting when we see it as relevant to our lives—and this is even more true for teenagers.

Adolescents are rightly wrapped up in themselves. They are engaged in an intense biological, psychological, and social journey. They are very much focused on trying to figure themselves out. If you want to teach them something, do it in a way that facilitates this search for self. Give them examples of people, places, and ideas that link what you are teaching to their own emotions, experiences, and identities. This technique is what psychoanalysts call "experience-near." Like nothing else, it will intrinsically motivate your students to seek understanding and learning.

Rely on Natural Consequences

Whenever possible, let your students experience the natural consequences of their behavior—whether losing points for turning a project in late or getting an A on an exam they studied hard for. If you've done a good job setting clear expectations, this will be easier on both your students and you, especially when their decision or behavior results in an unwanted outcome that you could fix for them.

Mistakes are a primary vehicle for learning and teenagers should be allowed to make them and live with the consequences. Needless to say, this is not the case for behaviors that threaten life or limb. But when they miss deadlines, skip class, neglect to study for a test, or don't do the reading, protecting them from the consequences of their poor decision by extending deadlines indefinitely, offering multiple make-up test dates, or simply "letting it go" without comment is not a kindness in the long run. The real kindness is in allowing them to take responsibility for their choices and behaviors now in the safety of middle school or high school, rather than in college or on the job when the consequences can be much more dire.

Experiencing natural consequences is not about punishment. Punishment at this age only gives students something else to rebel against. Or worse, it can cause them to shut down and shut us out. Imposing negative consequences tends to work only in the short run. It does not promote the kind of learning and growth we want for our students. It does not allow them to develop internally driven motivation to be better.

Harsh consequences imposed by an outside force may produce behavior changes, but they will be changes that need fear and intimidation to last. Natural consequences point kids in the right direction and result in genuine developmental progress.

Our goal as educators is to get our students to see themselves as the true authority figure in their own life. When we hold them accountable for their decision, we give them the opportunity to learn eventually that it's up to them to make good decisions for themselves and that it is possible for them to self-regulate.

Be Willing to Look for the Underlying Source(s) of Problem Behavior

When you do have a student who is acting out beyond "typical" adolescent behavior, or even struggling to meet a minor expectation, disapprove and respond firmly to the behavior but not the whole student. Ask yourself if this is normal limit-testing or whether there's more going on in the student's life or mind.

Consider the possibility of an underlying issue. (We will be exploring this in detail starting in Chapter 4.)

For instance, complicated relationships at home often play out at school. A student who feels disconnected or even alienated from their parents may take out their frustration on the nearest adult—which might be you.

Or maybe something less fraught is going on. Perhaps you have a student who is overwhelmed and exhausted by your homework assignments. You ask about how things are going, and the student reports taking two hours to complete assignments you think they should be able to do in half that time.

Today's students frequently take for granted their own "multitasking" or distracted studying. While those of us in Generation X might have listened to music while completing homework or maybe taken a phone call or two, today's students may be Snapping, scrolling through Instagram, and replying to DMs as they study. The answer here becomes helping them to monitor themselves. Suggest that they progress through their homework in timed increments (perhaps thirty to sixty minutes)—with scheduled breaks for checking social media.

Treat Them Like the Adults They Are Becoming

The best way to encourage adolescents' burgeoning maturity is to expect it, then act accordingly. Raise the bar where you can and many of your students will rise to meet it. Of course, the boundaries and expectations you have for eighth graders will be different than the ones you have for high school Seniors, but change the rules to accommodate greater expectations wherever you can. Let them try out their self-awareness, self-management, and judgment, and watch the impulsivity and risk-taking recede.

If You Are Yelling, You Are Losing

When I was a School Counselor, I was asked to give a talk to our school's parents on teenage development. At the time, my own daughter was around three years old. Intuitively, as I gathered my thoughts for the talk, I grabbed a book from my shelf that I thought might speak to and resonate with these parents of high schoolers. At the meeting, I held up the book and recommended it to them as a resource for navigating the next few years. The book is part of a well-regarded series by Louise Bates Ames and Frances Ilg titled, *Your Three-Year-Old: Friend or Enemy*. Their spontaneous, collective laughter told me that the parents understood the parallel point.

Adolescents are tackling comparable developmental challenges to what they faced as toddlers. This can be supremely challenging for the adults in their lives, but it is important that both parents and educators understand that it is normal, even necessary. And it's not personal. Psychologists consider rebellion a key task or "job" for adolescents.

Just as you would with a three-year-old, try to take your students' behavior in stride. (Or if you can't, make it look as if you are.) Meet them where they are. Give them safe boundaries in which to explore and come into their own. At the same time, let them know that no matter what they throw at you as a result of their impulsiveness and risk-taking, you are a sturdy presence in their lives. They can depend on you and all their teachers to have their best interests at heart, as they continue to seek out exactly what those interests might be.

Talk It Out: A Scenario and Questions for Discussion

Read through the scenario below. Then answer the questions that follow by yourself or with a group of colleagues.

You are sitting at your desk monitoring students working on their projects in small groups. Unexpectedly, you overhear one group of girls troubleshooting how to handle "requests for nudes." Instead of discussing their class project, these eighth graders are exchanging various techniques for taking such pictures and distributing them—techniques you're sure they learned on TikTok. From their conversation, you learn they've been receiving numerous requests from peers to share nude photos of themselves via text message and social media. The girls seem to be in respectful disagreement about both the meaning of these "requests" and how to handle them.

Discussion Questions

1 Developmentally speaking, how are these "requests" registering with these girls? What might they see as the reward(s)? What do they view (if anything) as the risk(s)? And how might this inform your response?
2 How do you understand the girls' primary needs here?
3 What else would you want to know if you found yourself in this situation? How might you obtain that information? Are there any barriers to gathering the information you need?
4 Would you consider pulling a colleague into the loop? If so, why and who?
5 Is there any need to involve a counselor or administrator at this point? On what criteria do you base this decision?
6 Is there any need to involve the student's families?
7 Are there any action steps you'll consider? Are there any barriers to taking these steps?
8 Is there anything you learn from handling this situation that speaks to an existing school policy, or might inform a new one?

Bibliography

1) Romer, A.L., Reyna, V.F., and Pardo, S.T. (2016) Are rash impulsive and reward sensitive traits distinguishable. A test in young adults. *Personality and Individual Differences* 99: 308–312.
2) Fed Up with Negative TikTok Challenges, Broward Schools Fight Back. (October 11, 2021) NBC Miami. https://www.nbcmiami.com/news/local/fed-up-with-negative-tiktok-challenges-broward-schools-fights-back/2571293/
3) Ames, Louise Bates and Ilg, Frances. (1980) *Your Three-Year-Old: Friend or Enemy.* Dell.

4

Worried, Sad, or Something More?

In the past year, 36.7% of high school students experienced persistent feelings of sadness or hopelessness. 18.8% seriously considered suicide.

– Centers for Disease Control: National Youth Risk Behavior Surveys (2019) https://www.childhealthdata. org/browse/survey/results?q=8183&r=1&g=828

An estimated 31.9% of children will experience an anxiety disorder by the age of 18.

– National Institutes of Healthhttps://www.nimh.nih. gov/health/statistics/any-anxiety-disorder#part_2578

The most common question I receive from teachers (and parents) is, "How do I know the difference between normal adolescent moodiness and something more serious?" My answer: It's not easy. But there are signs that can alert you that it's time to enlist professional help.

DOI: 10.4324/9781003358923-5

Teenagers are notorious among parents and teachers—even among themselves (see TikTok)—for being moody. When we view periodic irritability or dysphoria as a natural part of adolescence, attribute it to "hormones," and consider it a passing phase, we're speaking with scientific accuracy. As we've discussed, adolescents' developing brains and endocrine systems render them susceptible to emotional highs and lows. The demands of normal development during middle school (greater intellectual complexity, increased workload, and functional independence) followed by those of high school (emotional independence and the consolidation of identity) create a recipe for stress and reactive behaviors, even under the best of circumstances.

It's also scientifically accurate to state that during adolescence, the prevalence of virtually all mental health issues increases significantly—for biological, psychological, and social-cultural reasons. We do need to be attentive to this well-documented trend. Mood swings or difficulty regulating emotions are normal among middle- and high-school students. Yet, when irritability, fatigue, lack of motivation, or sadness become deep or persistent, we need to pay extra attention and consider whether more targeted, professional intervention is indicated.

As the title of this book points out, educators are often the first to notice a student's behavioral changes, the first to get an inkling that a student may be grappling with more serious vulnerability or distress. After all, at school, adolescents can't retreat to their bedrooms. You experience their behavior day in and day out, sometimes with closer seats and greater access than their parents. You observe their moment-to-moment responses as they navigate their way through classrooms, hallways, cafeterias, and playing fields. You become familiar with their "normal," so you can also tell when something is off.

As a high-school English teacher expressed to me,

A few years ago, I had this super quiet kid, a sophomore. Every day, he did his best to remain invisible. Then, one day he came to class with an attitude. He threw his paper on my desk and said something really rude. I took him straight to the counselor. I later found out he was suicidal.

She continued:

And last year, I had a kid in my AP (advanced placement) class who was just angry to be there. He'd sit at his desk, hands folded, signaling, 'I don't want to do this.' Then, one day he asked me to transfer him out of the AP section and into College Prep (a less academically challenging section). That got my attention. This is a really smart kid. I knew if he went to College Prep, he'd check out more. I started thinking, he's depressed. But I didn't know that for sure. I shared my perspective with him. I said, 'I'm thinking you belong in the AP class. Even if you haven't wanted to, you've shown me that you understand the material. Have you thought about this?' Then, I told him I was taking him to his counselor, who I knew would be a better judge of his state of mind.

In recounting this story to me, the teacher added, "We are not shrinks. We are not therapists. But at the same time, I can see when a kid is in trouble."

Neither of the above situations is unusual. Still, it's hard to know when—and how—to intervene. As we saw in the last chapter, psychosocial phenomena exist on a spectrum. As with any spectrum, the extremes can be easy to spot and call out. But most kids occupy some place in the messy middle. There's no bright line alerting us when their emotions and behaviors move from "normal and to be expected" to "serious and need-ing professional help." Further, what's normal behavior for one student—whether that's being defiant or exceptionally compli-ant—can be a sign of distress in another. The aim is to intervene well before a mental health issue results in behavior that could have life-altering consequences. The challenge is figuring out when that is.

Like I said, this isn't easy.

The Major Culprits

Depression and anxiety are the most common mental health issues in the general population—and adolescents are no exception. Overall, the rates of both anxiety and depression (including suicidal thoughts) have been on the rise in U.S. adolescents for at least a decade or so. With every year of age during adolescence, the likelihood of suffering from clinical depression or anxiety increases.

According to the Youth Risk Behavior Survey (YRBS), as of 2017, more than 31 percent of high-school students reported experiencing persistent feelings of sadness or hopelessness in the past year. According to the National Institute of Mental Health, roughly the same proportion of thirteen- to eighteen-year-olds will experience an anxiety disorder over the course of their adolescence. If you teach in high school or upper school, roughly one in four students in your classroom is likely to be struggling with anxiety or depression at this moment.

In 2021, with added pressures of a global pandemic on our young people, the American Academy of Pediatrics, the American Academy of Child and Adolescent Psychiatry, and the Children's Hospital Association declared a national state of emergency in child and adolescent mental health. Giving this emergency even more weight, depression and anxiety can feed off each other. One can—and often does—lead to and encourage the other.

In addition to world events, what drives depression and anxiety in middle and high schoolers varies by age and developmental stage. Sixth graders are most likely to worry about academic performance, as well as peer and teacher approval and acceptance. Testing and presentations can also make them especially anxious. In seventh and eighth grades, students continue to carry many of the same concerns, but add irrational, often intense or elaborate fears to them. Then in high school, they throw conflicts with their parents and existential worries into their mix of mental burdens (i.e., What's my purpose on this earth? What is the meaning of life?).

Rebecca, a remarkably well-adjusted eighth grader, came my way for a brief period due to some pandemic-related stressors. One day during our video session, she told me she had an "irrational fear" (her words) and wondered if I might help her deal with it.

She told me she'd been frightened by a trailer for a movie titled *Frozen*. "Not the one with Elsa and Anna, a different one," she said. This trailer showed the main characters talking a lift operator at a ski resort into letting them on the chairlift at the very end of the day. Halfway up the mountain, the chairlift comes to a halt. They're stuck. And nobody knows it. The operator is gone. No one else is around. They are left there to freeze!

"Ever since I saw the trailer," Rebecca said, "I keep worrying that that could happen to my family and me when we go skiing in a few weeks."

Her fear was indeed irrational—and also perfectly normal for her age. At thirteen years old, Rebecca was coming into her own as a sentient being with her own desires and more autonomy from both a cognitive and physical vantage point. It's an exciting time in life, but also scary.

So when she saw the trailer, Rachel's mind entertained the possibility that she herself might be clever enough to talk her way onto the ski lift at day's end, maybe even without her parents. What would happen to her? This shot at independence, for a kid Rebecca's age, is at once compelling and overwhelming. Thus, Rebecca's thoughts produced her obsessional, ruminative, phobic response as she tried to work out her own internal conflicts, which were rooted in her developmentally appropriate desires for autonomy.

While I didn't offer Rebecca anything like this deeper explanation, I did offer her some techniques for relieving her worry. She settled on thinking through the "worst case scenario" (which is never so bad once we think it through). She researched the likelihood that being left to freeze on a chairlift at a major resort could even happen. She then made plans—like having external chargers for everyone's phone while they ski—to be extra safe on the slopes. All good techniques to alleviate her anxiety on this trip, and all techniques she can use to self-soothe as she grows. In the end, the ski trip went smoothly. By the time Rebecca and I spoke again, she wasn't even sure what all the fuss had been about.

All students are going to grapple with peer pressure, tests, and big questions about life, as well as occasional irrational— where developmentally appropriate—worry or fear. Most will experience occasional sadness and worry as rational responses to difficult predicaments. And many, like Rebecca, will bounce back with some supportive conversation, problem-solving or coping strategies, and encouragement.

Some students, however, are going to be more sensitive, more prone to sadness and worry due to their temperament. These more deeply affected students are ripe for becoming overwhelmed by academic expectations, social snafus, and everyday demands. This can make them rather reactive, even when it doesn't appear to us that they are facing a particularly high level of external stress or impingement. Their emotional responses sometimes evolve into clinical depression and anxiety disorders. This is why you're keeping your eyes peeled.

Whether depression and anxiety are acting alone or together, they can interrupt development and negatively affect cognition and learning in well-documented, specific, and important ways. Even more frightening, left unchecked depression or anxiety can lead to self-harm and even death.

Depression

Depression is distinguished from common sadness or a "bad mood" by the duration of the mood state, as well as the presence of specific symptoms. In adults, these symptoms often are expressed as a subjective experience of sadness, hopelessness, reduced or heightened appetite, among others. Many depressed adults have trouble sleeping. Most also have the self-awareness to know their mood is out of the ordinary and that whatever is wrong is within their system. So, usually, they don't take their depression out on the world.

Many middle schoolers and some high schoolers don't have the mental ability to perceive or comprehend—let alone articulate—their own internal distress and underlying mood states. Though some might, most don't yet have the self-awareness (remember, that's an emerging skill) to recognize their sadness as something internal. While adults with depression turn inward, adolescents are more likely to turn outward and exhibit as defiant, irritable, and angry. Thus, adolescent depression often manifests in diminished academic performance or productivity. Some depressive symptoms tend toward different behavior patterns in adolescents than in adults. For example, depressed adults tend to have difficulty sleeping (insomnia), whereas depressed adolescents are more likely to feel tired and sleep more than usual.

Adolescents suffering with depression often exhibit low motivation, low energy, and poor concentration. They might suffer memory impairment, reduced executive functions, and slower thought processing. They may demonstrate a lack of doggedness in the face of a challenge, even when previously motivated and persistent. And sometimes they describe finding it difficult to get out of bed in the morning.

Again, looking at students as if they are miniature versions of us doesn't serve us or them adequately. In fact, it makes it easy for us to miss depression in adolescents much of the time. When viewed through our adult-centric lens, signs of depression in our students can be misread as indifference, laziness, and oppositionality—or dismissed as typical teen behaviors. As the adults in their lives, we must train ourselves to consider that sometimes with teenagers anger or other jarring behaviors might be masking a deep and persistent sadness that is marching toward depression.

Anxiety

Like depression, anxiety is a state everyone experiences at times. Anxiety is also one of those things you can't live with but can't live without. In her 2019 book, *Under Pressure: Confronting the Epidemic of Stress and Anxiety in Girls*, psychologist Lisa Damour describes the ways in which normal anxiety serves our students in constructive, adaptive ways. For example, if a student reports feeling anxious and also mentions they have a test coming up, Damour points out that their anxiety might be signaling them to study for the test so they'll feel prepared.

Damour also notes that normal anxiety can serve as an important signal of risk or danger to adolescents. She relates an anecdote about a girl in her practice who drank way too much at a party in response to feeling what at the time seemed like inexplicable social anxiety. In retrospect, during their session, the girl was able to understand that her anxiety was a signal that this party was actually not a comfortable or safe place for her to be. Damour helped her to see that her anxiety was rational and useful in that instance.

Like depression, however, anxiety can become a disorder when it is persistent, disproportionate, and irrational. People suffering with generalized anxiety worry about everything. They obsess about events that haven't happened. They often become preoccupied—for no logical reason—with the idea that they or someone they love is going to be harmed or die. To calm their worry and fear, they work to control their environment—and the people in it—to ensure predictable outcomes. As their anxiety worsens, activities designed to neutralize or quell it can fill up their lives.

Not surprisingly, a student who suffers with generalized anxiety disorder might not always say they are worried or nervous. They may present with an agitated or angry demeanor. They may report persistent headaches and stomachaches, and so frequent the nurse's office. Their preoccupation with worry may make them easily distractible or interfere with their sleep, so they arrive at school already exhausted. You might notice they stop participating in classroom discussion and activities, avoid tests, or—in extreme cases—start avoiding school altogether. Most cases of "school refusal" have some measure of severe anxiety at their root.

OCD, Panic, PTSD

Besides general anxiety, anxiety can present as obsessive-compulsive disorder (OCD), panic attacks, or post-traumatic stress disorder (PTSD).

A student with OCD will work to control their environment through repetitive or ritualistic behavior to alleviate whatever it is they fear. A student afraid of germs may wash their hands often. A student who fears chaos may arrange the items on their desk in the same way before every class. On the surface, you might say, so what? Hand washing or having a neat desk never hurt anyone. But someone with OCD does these behaviors to the point of interference with their daily routines or even harm. For instance, they wash their hands raw, or they become so preoccupied with the placement of objects on their desk that they can't pay attention in class. Their fears and the behaviors they generate are irrational. Like generalized anxiety, OCD can emerge organically (i.e., in response to a genetic or biological vulnerability, even a virus) and/or come about in response to painful psychological experiences or trauma.

Panic attacks, another manifestation of anxiety, come on suddenly and unexpectedly in the form of a physical "attack"—difficulty breathing, dizziness, chest pain, sweating. Panic attacks are often described by students as mimicking heart attacks. To be clear, they are not heart attacks, and medically they are harmless. Most only last for only a few minutes and dissipate over time with coping strategies. These attacks can be triggered by an environmental stressor (something the person fears) or by seemingly nothing at all, though there is usually an underlying, slow-building tension or anxiety that brings them about.

Once diagnosed, panic attacks—like the majority of anxiety disorders—can be treated and managed. But when one strikes a student out of the blue and they don't know what's happening, it's frightening and embarrassing if it happens in front of others. That fear and embarrassment can make the student even more anxious and cause them to further retreat into themselves.

PTSD is lingering anxiety caused by a significant, life-threatening event in the person's history or trauma caused by abuse over time. A student suffering with PTSD does not feel safe, even though they may be perfectly safe in the moment and the event that caused the trauma is no longer happening. To keep their fear at bay, students with PTSD work to circumvent anything that might trigger a memory of the trauma. This can be exhausting, life-consuming work.

Should their PTSD be triggered, students may react automatically—without control—usually with a fight, freeze, or flight response. This is why such a student can appear angry and volatile, distant, or unresponsive. Not surprisingly, the condition tends to interfere with the formation of trusting, close relationships—a critical developmental task for adolescents.

Again, while adults might have the self-awareness and fund of knowledge, to identify their PTSD, OCD, or panic disorder (or at least to say, "This does not seem normal!") and seek treatment, most adolescents do not. We have to be careful not to allow our adult-centric lens to dismiss their anxiety-driven behavior as merely indolence or defiance.

Signs They May Need Help

Once you've set aside your adult-centric lens, what exactly are you looking for? The following are behaviors that indicate a student might be heading toward depression, anxiety, or some more serious mental health issues:

- ♦ Loss of motivation.
- ♦ Loss of interest in schoolwork, sports, or other activities.
- ♦ Persistent, irrational irritability or anger.
- ♦ Persistent low energy.
- ♦ Persistent high energy—keyed up all the time with tense muscles.
- ♦ Increased sensitivity to rejection.
- ♦ Inability to focus.
- ♦ Changes in eating patterns (more or less).
- ♦ Changes in sleeping patterns (more or less).
- ♦ Signs of cutting or other self-injury.
- ♦ Reports of feeling sad, hopeless, depressed, or suicidal.

Also, take note if a student's mood state, fear, or worry is interfering with their daily activities, peer relationships, or academic performance. Along the same lines, notice if they are allowing their fears, sadness, or worries to make their decisions for them—perhaps they don't try out for a sports team when you know they want to or they drop out of a beloved club.

If a student's anxiety presents as a panic attack, there won't be any doubt that professional help is indicated. However, there won't be any time to call it in right then; you'll have to spring into service for the moment. So, here's what to do:

- ♦ Help the student sit down in private, if possible, with their feet on the floor.

- ◆ Ask whether this has ever happened before. If so, the student may recognize it as a panic or "anxiety" attack. If not, explain your suspicion that it may be a panic attack, that this sometimes happens to kids when they're stressed and can come "out of nowhere." *Focus on allaying fear. "This is symptom of anxiety and it won't harm you or your health."
- ◆ Reassure them that this will pass.
- ◆ Encourage them to slow their breathing when they can.
- ◆ Sit with them until the attack passes.
- ◆ Once it passes, reassure them this kind of reaction is common in adolescents and young adults—and is likely a passing phase for which treatment is available.
- ◆ Tell them they are fine and encourage them to return to class or whatever activity they were engaged in.
- ◆ Follow your school's protocol for reporting this type of incident.

While not wanting to overreact, when you are not sure what to do, err on the side of caution. Depression and anxiety evolve and can become more serious conditions with more serious consequences.

Don't Fly Solo

The decision about what to do with a student's potential mental health concern is not and should never be your responsibility alone. Don't fly solo—even if you're experienced, even if you think you've got this. No one should make these calls by themselves.

Ideally, your school has a protocol for educators to follow when it comes to a student's mental health and wellbeing. If yours does not, you should still refer the issue to the school counselor and an administrator. Let them discuss and decide the school's obligations, the student's best interest, whether and when to call parents, and what the next steps should be. This is not your area of expertise, and too much is at stake for this to be on you alone.

If the student has confided in you about a personal issue or their mental state, be sure they know that you cannot keep your conversation private if they reveal any risk to their safety—whether from someone else or themselves. Most students understand this principle. As a teacher, you are a "mandated reporter" and must notify the local department of child protection or social services if it's revealed to you that your student has been hurt or abused. However, you should not ever make a report on your own. Again, consult with your school counselor, social worker, dean, or another administrator. Let them determine how to proceed.

Also important to know, you can keep some of your student's secrets. For instance, it's fine to maintain student privacy about sadness over a breakup, dislike of another teacher, or other things students may choose to share with you, a trusted adult. If you're in doubt about what must be shared, consult a colleague without including identifying information about the student. This can be the school counselor, an administrator, or another teacher, if you are more comfortable with that. You might ask something like, "If a student told you X, how do you think you would handle it? Would you need to tell someone else? How would you approach it with your student?"

When it comes to informing parents (again go through your administration for this), my own rule is based on the following:

- ◆ Is there an ethical/legal obligation on the school's part to inform parents? (For instance, if a child is at physical risk, including from self-inflicted harm or has suicidal intent, the school must inform their parents.)
- ◆ For the many "gray areas" that arise with students, I ask myself, "If this were my child and the school knew X, and I later learned the information and discovered that the school kept it from me, how would I feel?"

If you do have to inform someone else, ask your student for their preference about how to handle this communication. A student may prefer to tell a parent on their own first and then have you follow up with a note or a phone call. Or, understanding that you need to inform the school counselor, some students will agree to meet with the counselor—maybe even have you accompany them. Most important is that you maintain your connection with the student and that you are transparent about whether you need to share their information, why you need to share it, and how and with whom you are going to share it.

If conducted discreetly and without judgment, bringing a student's issues to the attention of a professional can only help. Even if it turns out it's not clinical depression or an anxiety disorder after all, having an opportunity to work through a developmental challenge or life stressor with a caring counselor doesn't do any harm. Thankfully, mental health issues no longer carry the stigma they once did. On the whole, Generation Z students are much more comfortable talking about their mental health (see TikTok again) and asking for counseling or therapy than previous generations.

Still, it's good to remember that the level of comfort around mental health varies from one individual to another. There are also differences across American subcultures. In general, though, it is much easier to suggest mental health support to students (and to some extent, their parents) than it used to be. For most conditions, treatment (psychotherapy and perhaps medication) is widely available, though it may take significant effort and patience for a family to secure it.

Supporting Students with a Diagnosis

When one of your students has a documented psychiatric diagnosis, it's in both of your interests that you educate yourself on their issue. Gaining some understanding of their mental health condition allows you to support the student in your classroom or advisory, on the team you're coaching, or when you're on lunch duty in the cafeteria. No one is better positioned to flag potential challenges for a student and offer practical solutions than an educator who knows what the student is up against.

I worked with a high-school student who had a significant fear of eating in public settings—a form of Social Phobia, which is a category of anxiety disorder. Though she was extremely social and had many friends, she couldn't bring herself to get food in the dining hall at lunchtime, let alone sit at a communal table and eat it. Learning of her issue and knowing she was working on it in therapy, one of her teachers made his office available to her and one of her close friends at lunchtime. The friend would grab food for both of them, and they ate in the teacher's office each day privately. With that simple gesture, the teacher eliminated some of the student's anxiety—paving the way for better results in therapy and school.

And I'll never forget a quiet, rather elusive student named Rowan, from my early days as a school counselor. Rowan walked through the school's hallways with his hood up, an overgrown shock of sandy hair protruding out from it, headphones always in his ears. He had an air of cool discontent (or was it angst?), though he never called much attention to himself.

Following reasonably successful ninth and tenth grade years, as an eleventh grader Rowan stopped turning his work in on time—or at all. The high quality of the assignments he did manage to turn in demonstrated his intellectual strength. Time management and efficiency, however, were not in his wheelhouse.

At a faculty meeting, Rowan's teachers commiserated about how difficult it was to "do business" with him. "He's slippery," one teacher quipped. "The other day I asked him to wait after class so we could talk about the project he needs to complete. But once class ended, he got up from his desk and somehow snuck right out the door."

Another teacher described how Rowan failed to appear for requisite office hours to go over his term-paper plan. "He is just hard to catch," she said. "A lot of the time it seems like he is avoiding responsibility." (By the way, here is a wonderful example of adults looking at an adolescent's behavior through their adult lens. Their tone also suggested the teachers were taking Rowan's behavior personally and regarding it as a sign of disrespect.)

Rowan was not outwardly distressed. He wasn't disrupting classes or anything. Any of his behaviors by themselves could be described as typical for his age. Was Rowan being lazy? Oppositional? Or was there something more? Perplexed, his teachers look to me for input.

As was often my experience as a school counselor, my colleagues were most interested in, if not a full clinical assessment, some piece of actionable advice. Our team decided that I'd meet with Rowan's parents to see what we might learn about what was happening at home.

Upon sitting down with Rowan's parents, I quickly learned that they were at their wit's end, as well. They'd had no results from reminding him to do his homework and turn it in. Further, they said he didn't speak to them much, preferring to spend time alone in his room. They did mention, in passing, that Rowan was seeing a therapist.

Eager for more information, I requested their permission and Rowan's to call his therapist. Over the phone, the therapist confirmed that Rowan had been very hard to reach when she first met him and that his relationship with his parents was far from ideal. She told me she'd come to know Rowan well over the months they'd worked together and become quite fond of him. She then confirmed what his teachers suspected: Rowan had some organizational weaknesses, as well as a mild case of attention deficit disorder (ADD). The ADD made it hard for him to manage the increased workload in eleventh grade. But, she added, neither of those were his big issues. "It's anxiety," she said. "That's why he's avoiding his teachers and unable to get the help he needs. Rowan has the worst case of Social Phobia I've ever seen."

With that, we had a diagnosis. "Social Phobia" is a specific anxiety disorder in which routine social interactions cause irrational fear and self-consciousness. It is not the same as shyness or social awkwardness. It can occur in those who are neither shy nor awkward. Social Phobia's primary symptom is an intense fear of situations in which one might be judged (like meeting with a teacher about an overdue assignment) or inadvertently offend someone. Adolescents with this diagnosis worry such situations might end in embarrassment or humiliation. They describe having thoughts such as, "Nobody likes me," "I am going to say something stupid," "I'm going to embarrass myself the minute I open my mouth."

While this may sound like run-of-the-mill teenage insecurity (what sixteen-year-old doesn't feel like this sometimes?), the duration of it and the disruption it was causing in Rowan's life made it a diagnosable condition. Rowan wasn't just reacting, then gradually pulling himself out of it. His brain was constantly entertaining a set of recurring, automatic thought patterns that affected his decisions and resulted in him avoiding normal social interaction.

Rowan was terrified of disappointing his teachers, which made him so exquisitely self-conscious about everything he said and did that he could not bring himself to talk with them. Yet, the academic demands of the school required that Rowan engage with his teachers. It was, of course, the only way he could get help managing both the structure and content of his work.

On the advice of Rowan's therapist—and with Rowan's and his parents' permission—I explained his diagnosis and contextualized his behavior to his teachers. I told them he was avoiding them not because he is indifferent but because he cares so deeply about what they think of him.

Given how cool and "above it all" Rowan seemed, it hadn't occurred to his teachers (or me) that he suffered from Social

Phobia, let alone that he was intimidated by them. Once my colleagues understood what was behind Rowan's behavior, they were less impatient and more empathic.

I told my teacher colleagues that the therapist recommended that when they wanted to talk with Rowan that they should avoid scheduling a meeting or making plans with him. That would only give him time to grow so anxious about the interaction that he'd feel compelled to run from it. From now on, they should simply approach him and say what they need to say.

Also at his therapist's suggestion, I reached out to Rowan to let him know that his teachers would be proactively addressing him on the spot when they needed to meet with him. He was agreeable to this, acknowledging that he was in fact terribly afraid of letting his teachers down and that as soon as he fell behind on an assignment, he felt unable to face them.

I can't say that Rowan's path from there was perfect or even smooth. But once his teachers better understood the type of anxiety driving his behaviors—and he knew that they knew—they were able to work together. The tension and frustration were reduced for all parties, including Rowan.

Situations like Rowan's reflect how very difficult it is to assess others' motivations and inner experiences from the outside. Even as an experienced School Counselor, I couldn't see under the surface in the school setting. I needed a more specialized, comprehensive outside opinion to inform my understanding and planning. While this is true of the general human experience, it is especially true when it comes to adolescents.

Having a Plan

Throughout this chapter, I have been alluding to a school protocol to help you and your colleagues know what to do if you suspect a student may be having mental health issues. If your school doesn't have a written protocol for managing mental health issues, you should strongly suggest they write one.

No school and no teacher is immune from being confronted by mental health issues. In these situations, every teacher wants to know that any action they take is the correct thing to do and in the best interest of the student. Every school wants to ensure best practices and avoid liability issues. Every parent wants to know the right thing is being done for their child. Having clear guidelines to look to relieves the pressure on everyone.

In addition to a protocol, your school might also look into creating a mental health safety net. Depending on the school's resources and the nature of the student and family population, some things to consider include:

A Multidisciplinary Team

This team—made up of the school nurse, counselor, advisor, dean, division head, classroom teacher, health-wellness educator, coach, consulting psychiatrist—is charged with managing a student's issues where school is concerned. For instance, they might make sure all needed services are secured, any diagnoses affecting the student's academics is discussed, and solutions are found. They can also monitor the student's progress.

Peer Counselor or Listener Programs

Adolescents feel more comfortable confiding in their peers. A peer counseling or listener program takes advantage of this developmental feature. Peer counselors can be specially trained to help their fellow students with everyday problems, while listening for concerning situations that need adult attention. To learn more about this, peer support training manuals can be found at:

- ◆ Certified Peer Educator (CPE) Training, NASPA.org.
- ◆ Anne Ford's Peer Support Manual, https://connectpeersupport.com/publications/#manual.
- ◆ Kathryn & David Geldard's Adolescent Peer Support Training Manual, https://www.yumpu.com/en/document/read/13913255/adolescent-peer-counsellor-training-manual-kathryn-david-geldard.

Karen Gross's "Generation T" (for Trauma)

The reasons mental health issues are on the rise today among students are all too obvious to all of us. Social media, of course, fosters greater social comparison, most of it negative. Electronic communication, among other things, leads to lack of adequate sleep. Their parents, too, are more stressed, depleted, isolated, and concerned for their children's future. Throw in a global pandemic that closes schools (student's primary social outlet and source of structure) along with climate change, frequent school shootings, and a renewed threat of nuclear war, and what is clear is that our children today live with so many uncertainties beyond their control—some of which are life threatening and show no signs of relenting.

In her 2020 book, *Trauma Doesn't Stop at the School Door: Strategies and Solutions for Educators, Pre-K – College*, educator Karen Gross writes:

> [This generation] … has experienced outsized trauma that has been and is person caused and nature caused. It starts with 9/11 and those in school then may now be in post-secondary education. We have had hurricanes and fires and school shootings and bombings; places of historic safety (houses of worship, marathons, movie theaters, outdoor concert venues, for example) are the sites and places of vicious attacks.
>
> The enrolled students since 9/11 have experienced trauma—as have their families. And that trauma is carried into the educational system, often in invisible backpacks. And that trauma has impacted learning, psychosocial development, and health/wellness now and into the future. This generation is not based on birth years: it is premised on their being in school during decades of trauma.

School counselors and outside mental health professionals, including pediatricians, are, of course, essential to helping adolescents learn to manage and maintain their mental health through the challenges of their times and as they grow toward adulthood. But you, their teacher, more often than not are going to be the one who gets the ball rolling.

So, what do you do if you're not sure whether it's normal adolescent moodiness or something more serious? First, remember that you are an educator, not a mental health care professional. Then take off your adult-centric lens, trust your instincts, follow your school's protocol, and advocate for your students, as always.

A Supportive Environment

An easy, cost-free, and practical thing to do is put up a very visible list of resources for mental health education and support in your school counselor's or dean's office—or both. This not only informs students who don't want to talk where they can get help on their own, it also signals that the school is open, supportive, and a safe space in which to address mental health issues.

Some resources to list might include:

♦ The Steve Fund (specifically for high-school and college students of color), stevefund.org.
♦ The Trevor Project (specifically for LGBTQ youth), thetrevorproject.org.
♦ Jed Foundation (for high-school and college students), jedfoundation.org.
♦ Lifeline, a suicide prevention hotline, 1-800-273-8255.
♦ 988, a new three-digit dialing code that routes U.S. callers, texters, or chatters to the National Suicide Prevention Lifeline (as of July 16, 2022) and a trained counselor in their network.
♦ Crisis Text Line, crisistextline.org.

- ◆ Headspace, headspace.com.
- ◆ Mindshift, anxietycanada.com/resources/mindshift-cbt/.
- ◆ Calm, calm.com.

You might also have your school counselor look into mood and anxiety apps for teenagers that they can recommend.

Talk It Out: A Scenario and Questions for Discussion

Read through the scenario below. Then answer the questions that follow by yourself or with a group of colleagues.

Emily is a twelfth grader in your AP calculus class. You also taught her in ninth grade, and you've come to know her fairly well over the past few years. She's been an increasingly strong, even driven, math student. She's diligently sought help from you when she's needed it. A couple of times, Emily has become tearful over a (relatively) low quiz grade. But she's always pulled it together once you've conveyed your confidence in her. A versatile and multi-talented student, Emily was accepted to her dream school as an early decision applicant. Shortly thereafter, she mentioned to you she's considering pursuing a math major.

Upon return from spring vacation, however, Emily seems distracted, even disengaged. Usually an attentive, enthusiastic student, she doesn't seem interested or even that present in class. As you're chatting in the teachers' lounge, your colleague, who teaches English and with whom you share a number of students, begins venting to you about some of the twelfth graders who seem to have "checked out." It may be predictable, but it's still just as annoying every year. And by the way, what's up with Emily? She really seems to have declared a full-on senior slump. I know you know her pretty well, and she looks up to you. Have you thought about calling her out on the slump situation?

Discussion Questions

1 What do you think might be going on with Emily? What do you think about your colleague's comment?
2 What else would you want to know if you found yourself in this situation? How might you obtain that information?
3 How do you believe you can best serve the needs of the student in this situation?
4 Might there be any barriers to engaging this student?
5 If you've ever found yourself in a comparable situation, how did it turn out? What did you learn and how did you learn it?

Bibliography

1) Damour, Lisa. (2019) *Under Pressure: Confronting the Epidemic of Stress and Anxiety in Girls*. Ballantine Books.
2) Gross, Karen. (2020) *Trauma Doesn't Stop at the School Door: Strategies and Solutions for Educators, Pre-K – College*. Teachers College Press. Columbia University.

Section II
Social Contexts

5

Race, Ethnicity, and Culture

> I wish my teachers understood that I am not fully Asian nor am I fully American … I fall somewhere on a spectrum, as do many [Asian-American students]. Although our experiences are shared, we each have a really distinct and unique story.
>
> – Eleventh grader

If you teach in a predominantly white school, you may know a student like Isaac. A Black graduate of a New England boarding school who is currently a college junior, he reflects on his high-school experience in the following way:

> I think because I was Black and a recruited athlete, less was expected of me academically. My class—and the whole school—saw me as kind of a mascot. And I played into it. I mean, I took on the role, tried to make people laugh. And people took me even less seriously.

DOI: 10.4324/9781003358923-7

With further psychological development and a couple of years at a large, relatively diverse university, Isaac can now see how his racial identity influenced the way many of his teachers and classmates seemed to perceive him. Further, he has come to recognize how their perceptions affected how he saw himself at that time. For Isaac, his race was the primary factor in why, at least in his perception (which sounds accurate), teachers saw him as lacking intellectual potential or strength.

I would argue that Isaacs's gender—and perhaps the fact that he was recruited to the school as a basketball player—intersected with his race here, too. It's possible his family's status as low-income in an affluent school community was also an identity about which people made assumptions, though it's hard to know for sure.

It was only sometime well post-graduation that he was able to reflect on how he was seen and the role his own acceptance of bias may have played. Today, Isaac is thoughtful and candid in acknowledging that—at least at times—he responded to others' perceptions by internalizing and fulfilling them, to his own detriment.

Diversity, Equity, Inclusion and Belonging (DEIB) refers to an increasingly prominent approach in schools to recognize and respect differences among students (diversity), to provide each student with the resources and support they need in order to give them equal footing (equity), and to make sure everyone is not only accepted but welcomed in the community regardless of their race, ethnicity, religion, sexual orientation, and gender identity (inclusion and belonging).

Race and ethnicity are primary drivers of DEIB efforts because they are so frequently a source of bias, discrimination, social exclusion—as well as violence—for students. Even honest, wholly unintended missteps—for example, a white teacher repeatedly mixing up the names of the only two Black girls or Asian-American boys in the class—can inadvertently cause emotional harm.

Perspective

Speaking to issues of race and ethnicity as a white person—and a Generation X-er at that—is a complicated proposition. I have neither the lived experience of a person of color nor the academic expertise that I have about my own field of adolescent psychology. That said, I believe that any discussion of adolescent development, identity, and mental health must touch upon race and ethnicity if it is to maintain relevance and integrity. I will use this space not to profess my expertise, but to share what I am learning.

According to the Pew Research Center, Generation Z is the most racially and ethnically diverse generation to date in the United States. More Generation Z students identify as biracial, multiracial, and/or bicultural than any previous generation. And anyone who teaches or works with today's students also knows that they are more aware of and attuned to racial and ethnic identity.

While students and families from what have traditionally been termed "racial minorities" in the United States have been acutely aware of race and ethnicity for a long time, those in this new generation have ready access to information—and to other students of various races and cultures—not just in their midst but across the country and the globe. Thus, today's middle- and high-school students often demonstrate a more nuanced, confident understanding of racial issues than their parents. In fact, many white students, who in previous generations may have thought little about race— because theirs did not disadvantage them—are thinking and talking about race and ethnicity more openly and thoughtfully. Though racism remains a pervasive and dangerous problem, many students are challenging it as well (an adaptive use of a developmental tendency).

Whatever their identity, today's students are coming of age in a time of intense identity politics, racialized violence, and renewed racial activism. Racial and ethnic tensions—within the country and perhaps in their local communities—are embedded in our students' minds and environments. While this is all swirling around them, your adolescent students are at a developmental stage (as we discussed in Chapter 2) where they're hard at work defining their identities. A major part of that process—particularly for Black, Asian-American/Pacific Islander, Latinx, and Native/Indigenous students—is a growing awareness of their race and ethnicity: what it is, where and how it fits, what it means to them.

As educators, we need to pay particular attention when a student identifies as a person of color, i.e., a member of a racial minority group. (I am using "Person of Color" in the broadest sense here to refer to any and all non-white students.) This identity has consequences—both positive and negative—for their mental health and wellbeing, as well as their feelings of belonging, self-esteem, and expectations. This is particularly salient for students of color in predominantly white schools.

We serve our students and their educational needs most effectively when we get to know the "whole student." By reflecting and considering how race and cultural issues affect our students' perceptions of themselves, others, and the world around them, we gain a deeper understanding of their thoughts and reactions—placing ourselves in a better position to know when something is wrong and what kinds of contextual variables may contribute to problems and solutions. Understanding where students are coming from and the place they occupy in the world, as well as in our school, enables us to communicate more effectively with them about algebra, writing, chemistry … their relationships and wellbeing. When students feel fully seen and understood, it lowers the risk for misunderstandings, hurt feelings, and anger.

When a student presents a psychological or behavioral issue, our ability to offer an emotionally safe environment that is, at the very least, aware of and sensitive to racial-ethnic identity, can be essential. This is especially true when our identities and those of our students @ differ in ways that reflect power and status beyond that of an adult professional and an adolescent student. This is most often the case if you are a white teacher working with a non-white student.

While I work with students from a diverse set of racial and cultural backgrounds, the bulk of my professional experience has been concentrated in white-majority schools and communities. Thus, many of the observations in this chapter are based on student experiences in such environments—those of both students of color and white students. Therefore, I cannot speak from direct knowledge to students' experiences in schools where students of color constitute the majority population.

Who Am I?

The foundation of our identity—who we believe we are—is shaped first by our experiences within our family. As we grow, societal forces and how we experience the world around us, build on that foundation. How we react to the world and how the world reacts to us further determines how we perceive ourselves.

Whatever our generational membership, our own racial and ethnic identity has evolved over time as a function of psychosocial development and changing contexts and historical moments. If you are a person of color, a person born outside the United States, or a first-generation member of an immigrant family—in other words, not part of the "majority" or dominant U.S. population—your racial and cultural identity may have been salient for you since childhood or adolescence.

Growing up in a relatively homogenous, white community, I did not consciously experience my whiteness or my culture as significant parts of my identity as a child—though they very much were. It wasn't until I went to college and met students with other racial identities and cultural backgrounds that I began to recognize the meaning and place of my own race and ethnicity.

Over the decades since college, the meaning I extract from my racial and cultural identity has continued to shift and evolve, largely in response to new personal and professional relationships and insights gained in conversation, as well as to evolving professional and historical contexts. Contrary to popular belief, identity development is not "finished" or "complete" once we reach adulthood, though it is during adolescence that, like so many things, it's on center stage.

What's in Your Inner Circle?

While teaching a college course in adolescent psychology, I had my students fill out an "identity wheel" worksheet. On each sheet was a list of identity categories: gender, race, ethnicity, age, sexual orientation, education, income, religion, political beliefs, work experience, etc. Next to the list were two circles, one within the other. Students were instructed to put the identities they related to most in the inner circle and identities that were less important to them in the outer circle. When they were finished, I had them split up into small groups and discuss what they'd learned about themselves.

As I walked around the room and visited each group, I noted that all the international students or students of color invariably placed their ethnic and racial identity prominently in that inner circle. One Filipino-American female student stated proudly that she "a hundred percent" related to being Asian—and "within the category of Asian, Filipino." All the white students, on the other hand, placed gender, religion, or sexual orientation in their inner circles. Not one of them emphasized their whiteness.

It's important to note here that while white students in a majority white environment may never mention their race—and don't keep it in forefront of their minds as an identity—their racial and cultural identity (and all that comes with it) are still very much a part of how they see themselves and how they relate to the world.

Intersectionality

Identity, of course, is more complex than one or two factors. In 1989, legal scholar and civil rights activist Kimberlé Crenshaw, today a professor of law at UCLA and Columbia University, coined the term "intersectionality" to describe how various aspects of our identities (race, class, gender, religion, disability) intersect and overlap to result in social injustice on varying levels. This is especially true of those intersecting identities that relate to privilege, marginalization, and discrimination—such as race and cultural background. These overlapping identities shape our life experience and color both how we encounter and respond to every interaction we engage in.

Crenshaw first devised the term as a frame for explaining bias and violence against Black women. Over the years, it has proven useful as a broader, more comprehensive frame to understand how and why the same situation can be interpreted differently by different people.

When the video of George Floyd, an unarmed Black citizen, being murdered by Derek Chauvin, a white former Minneapolis police officer, went viral in May 2020, it seemed to be all anyone was talking about across the country. Our schools were no exception. Each of our reactions to this horrifying event, any comment we made, any action we took was filtered through our identities—and in this case most especially, through our racial and cultural identities.

In the final weeks of spring semester that year, my patient Ava, a Black student in a white-majority high school, was confused and feeling isolated. She found herself compelled to watch the video of Floyd's murder repeatedly, even though she felt vicariously traumatized each time she did. Compounding her trauma was the fact that—as her mother pointed out to me—George Floyd's physical appearance (his skin tone, his build, some of his facial features) was remarkably similar to that of Ava's father.

Our unique personal identities affect how we process a situation, determine what's happening, and respond. The same is true for our students. A white student doesn't have the same experience as a Black student who doesn't have the same experience as a Latinx student, etc. And students from within the same racial identity don't necessarily have the same experience as each other. Everyone operates with a unique set of identities. Though many of her white classmates were disturbed and outraged by George Floyd's murder, they simply couldn't experience it in the personal way Ava did. When she was at school, she told me, she felt alone with her grief and fear.

Not surprisingly, it was a teacher who first observed something. She noticed that Ava was uncharacteristically agitated and distracted in class. Putting two and two together, she recognized that maybe the non-stop news coverage of George Floyd's murder and the nightly protests growing from it might be affecting Ava differently from her white peers. Because they had a close, positive relationship, Ava's teacher reached out and asked Ava if she'd like to chat during a lunch period.

Taking her teacher up on the offer, Ava talked readily about recent events and her difficulty talking about it with classmates, and to a certain extent even her own parents. Her teacher—who was white—did not interject her own opinions. She simply acknowledged and validated Ava's feelings.

Following the conversation with her teacher, as well as talks with one trusted friend, Ava got involved with the growing racial justice movement by attending a local demonstration. She also decided to circulate an online petition in her school demanding justice for George Floyd.

Had Ava's teacher not supported her, I'm not sure she would have been as resilient as she was. I am sure she would not have had the confidence to circulate the petition among her classmates, a couple of whom used the contact as a vehicle to approach her to talk about the situation.

It can't have been easy for Ava's teacher to reach out to her. She happened to be an older white woman who had loads of experience and resultant confidence from years of teaching. However, she did not have any specific expertise in racial identity or race relations. I, for one, relate to her and appreciate the risk she took. Her effort could have landed poorly, or even backfired. But I sense that she knew Ava (and perhaps herself) well enough to step forward.

Most of us who came of age in the previous century have responded in various ways to specific events, as well as changing dialogue around race and other key issues of social identity over the decades. As a white, American, cisgender, Generation X woman from a professional family, I've been shaped by my childhood context, my educational opportunities, and the way that environment has responded to me. I've experienced sexism—in institutionalized ways, such as being excluded from Little League baseball because I was a girl, and in informal ways that reflect power differentials, such as being treated in a condescending or sexualized manner by male professor or boss. But I've never been subject to racism.

Commenting to me about her conversation with her teacher, Ava made this salient observation about the teacher's approach:

> She didn't act like I was supposed to be the expert for all Black people or even all Black kids. She asked me how I was reacting and what I thought. I mean, obviously I am Black, and I knew that's why she was asking me, but it didn't come off weird or racist. I actually appreciated it.

So when, as a psychologist, I work with students, like Ava, who've had negative, even traumatic lived experiences due to their racial or cultural identities, I listen for the different, particular nature of their experiences. I also try not to make assumptions. Still, I'm amazed by how many I make.

I Didn't Know You Were...

Physical appearance does not always tell the whole story. I hear from students whose appearance does not conform to a common notion of what members of a particular ethnic or racial group "look like" that it can be difficult and confusing when classmates and teachers are surprised to learn who they are. It happens to adults, too.

A very light-skinned Indian colleague of mine was a featured speaker at his school's faculty meeting on diversity, equity, and inclusion. He addressed his colleagues and spoke openly about his personal identity and his experiences growing up in an immigrant family.

After the talk, another teacher—a friendly, collegial white man some years his senior—exclaimed, "I didn't know you were Indian!" This was not the first time this sort of thing had arisen my colleague's life. He was good-natured about it in the moment. But later to me, he said it pulled him right back into the feeling of not being fully seen or known, the feeling he had all the time while growing up in a largely white community.

Because I've heard about experiences like that of my colleague, when I find myself "surprised" to learn someone's identity, i.e., that it's different from what I assumed (for example, a very light-skinned, "white-presenting" student or colleague who actually has a South Asian or Latinx ethnicity), I try to keep the surprise to myself and also take note that people are not always as they appear to us.

Even when we think we have a reasonably clear impression of a student's identity, it takes work and mindfulness to resist injecting our experiences into our interpretation of their experiences. Don't judge yourself too harshly for this. It's only natural, as we want and need to relate to what students tell us. But be aware of this very human tendency.

Interestingly, we may be more prone to falling into this trap when we share a student's racial or ethnic identity. It is, after all, wonderful and powerful for kids to know we "get it" at the level of lived experience. But sometimes experiences within a comparable identity can be really different.

I recently encountered this very phenomenon. Abby, a Jewish college student in my private practice, was telling me about an argument she was having with her mother. Her mother was insisting Abby attend a consultation with a plastic surgeon about getting a "nose job" while she was home for the summer. Abby, an awkward high schooler who was having newfound romantic success on her college campus, was feeling confident about her appearance and, perhaps relatedly, disinterested in surgically altering the shape of her nose.

As Abby spoke, my mind began to register all the ways such a demand from a parent could be harmful to a young adult. Unfortunately, I was not stealthy with my concern. Though I said nothing, Abby could read my face and began to reassure me (not something a counselor aims for). "I mean, it's not a big deal," she said. "It's kind of a rite of passage for Jewish girls from New York to get nose jobs."

While, like Abby, I am Jewish and was aware of the "rite" she described, I can honestly say that this practice—to undergo plastic surgery, as a matter of course—was in no way normalized in my family of origin nor in my current mindset. Thus, I contextualized her mother's request very differently than Abby did.

You can come from the same culture or subculture as a student or patient and still have a really different experience of what's "normal." It's easy to assume that because you're from the same culture you understand each other. And sometimes this is absolutely true. But sometimes it's not. For Abby, the nose job pressure was normal, while I was dismayed that a mother would put this kind of appearance enhancement and conformity pressure on her daughter.

If we want to understand our students—especially when they're struggling—sometimes we need to quiet our own identities (and experiences) in order to listen to them. We need to stay open and curious, so we can see their situation through their eyes.

Bias Is a Two-Way Street

Staying open and curious is an optimal and useful stance. However, such a stance is hard to maintain. The big hurdle here is bias. Our biases are the products of our identity and our experiences. Biases come in two primary types: explicit and implicit.

Explicit biases are those preferences that are in our consciousness, ones we are aware of. For instance, when we make a conscious choice to top our pizza with pepperoni and not anchovies, we demonstrate an explicit bias for pepperoni and an explicit bias against anchovies.

Implicit biases are those preferences that are so ingrained in us we no longer notice or question them. They fly under the radar of our consciousness. They are likely shaped by both explicit and implicit messages we take in from cultural sources like movies, advertisements, and the distinct culture and beliefs of our own families of origin. For example, we may think curly hair is most desirable, place a high value on education, or always reach for the same brand of ketchup in the grocery store.

For the most part, our implicit biases make our brains—and our lives—more efficient. After all, making a conscious decision about which brand of ketchup to buy every time you go to the grocery store would be cumbersome.

Implicit biases become an issue when they causes us to act on preferences that are out of alignment with our values and ambitions—such as making assumptions about people based on the color of their skin or their ethnic background. Such biases are typically established in our thought patterns by the culture in which we were raised. Whether or not they are pronounced, they are there at work in the background of our lives until we recognize and, ultimately, reflect on and evaluate them.

Again in her book, *Why Are All the Black Kids Sitting Together in the Cafeteria?*, psychologist Beverly Tatum captures the essence of prejudice:

> Prejudice is one of the inescapable consequences of living in a racist society. Cultural racism—the cultural images and messages that affirm the assumed superiority of Whites and the assumed inferiority of people of color—is like smog in the air. Sometimes it is so thick it is visible, other times it is less apparent, but always, day in and day out, we are breathing it in.

For this reason alone, racial and cultural differences should be addressed as a factor that affects classroom and campus interactions and dynamics. Some people are consciously biased against people who are different from them. But for most of us, our racial and cultural biases are implicit.

In the classroom, implicit bias might work like this: We may think we're judging a student fairly—whether positively or negatively—based on observed behaviors. But at times an implicit bias based on our own identity and/or that of our student may have led us to automatically make up our mind about them. It's only after that automatic thought makes our decisions for us that our brain goes searching for "observed facts" to support our conclusion and justify our thinking.

To complicate matters, that student brings their own set of assumptions and implicit biases to the interaction. In cases such as Isaacs's, which opened this chapter, this can even create a self-fulfilling prophecy.

We all fall victim to our implicit bias—the tricky part is that we usually have no idea when we are judging people or situations without the facts. Our false assumptions lead to false conclusions, which can lead to ill-informed and thus poor decisions and actions.

One student, Jack, made this abundantly clear to me in a very concrete way. He was a white student attending a racially and economically diverse boarding school. At his school, many of the white students were from wealthier families, while many of the Black students were not. This was a statistical fact on this particular campus, though also a common stereotype. One day in our individual session, he reported to me that his classmates inaccurately perceived his circumstances. "People think I'm rich, because I'm white," he said.

Jack was from a very low-income, single-parent household. But I also suspected that his peers not only thought he was rich because he was white (a common stereotype related to another one: that Students of Color are always from low-income communities or receiving scholarships), but also because he consistently wore what I recognized to be exceedingly expensive, designer clothes.

When I mentioned Jack's statement, juxtaposed with my observations of his high-end wear, to his school counselor, I got an unexpected and rather alarming response. "Oh, yes, he does have nice clothes," the counselor told me. "They're hand-me-downs. His mother works as a housekeeper for a family with a son a few years older than Jack. Her employer gives Jack's mom all of her son's outgrown clothes."

Once again, I learned in a surprising way that it's difficult and unrealistic to think we can judge a book by its cover.

Fortunately, we can check our implicit bias by slowing down our thought process. All it takes is pausing our thoughts long enough to ask ourselves, "What kinds of assumptions or stereotypes might be influencing my perceptions or behavior?" This gives our brains more time to come online with clearer thinking.

The trick is catching your implicit bias in action. I do this by trying to notice any time I make a declaration that a student (or anyone) is this way or that way. When that happens, before I accept my thought, I ask myself, "What is my evidence?" Then, just to be sure, I see if I can entertain the opposite thought. That usually gives my brain the break it needs to check my bias. (By

rt Affinity Groups

exis's school does, your school can encourage and support
y groups. These groups create a designated, emotionally
ace for students who share a particular identity—usually in
way vulnerable or marginalized. The group allows them to
together to speak candidly about their experiences. It frees
or a time from the pressures of assimilation to the dominant
e and from real or perceived judgment of majority peers.
metimes affinity groups occur naturally—in that students
omparable racial or ethnic backgrounds seek each other
ut when they are organized more formally, students who
e outside a certain friend group or at another grade level
el more welcome.
finity groups at the high-school level are often student-ini-
and do not necessarily include or require faculty or staff in
eetings. Others are sponsored or managed by a teacher, a
ty director, or another administrator.

ge Diversity-Equity-Inclusion-Belonging (DEIB) Training
at part of the professional development time for faculty
ff be devoted to DEIB training.

our Course Material for Bias
own high-school, undergraduate, and graduate experi-
he majority of the textbooks and other books we read were
by white men from privileged backgrounds. I'm guessing
e was true of your education. White identity, white cul-
d white experience is often the "default" in classes from
e (just look at the table of contents of any anthology) to his-
the sciences. It's not only limiting, but students who aren't
nd/or privileged can't see themselves or their experiences
in what they're reading or in class discussion.
ringing diverse points of view to your course content, you
the breadth of your students' education, their experience,
r critical thinking skills no matter the subject you teach.

the way, it's really hard—though not necessarily impossible—for our students to do this. Remember, their frontal lobes are developing as we speak.)

It also helps to invest some time in reckoning with your own racial and cultural identities. Become familiar with how your personal background and identity interface with those of your students and your colleagues. This will provide clues as to where your implicit bias may be strongest. Do this and all things around identity with curiosity and self-acceptance—and without judgment. Remember—we're all products of our experiences and the biases we've developed. There's always room for new understanding and growth.

It may feel overwhelming to think about ourselves as biased because it sounds and feels like we are prejudiced, bigoted, even destructive or malicious. The fact is our minds are both consciously and unconsciously contending with societal messages about others—and ourselves—as we go about our daily lives. We can't erase or even ignore these messages. But by recognizing they exist, we take a step toward giving them less control and less capacity affect how we behave.

Code-switching

Alexis is a Black student at a predominantly white, private school where I consult. She lives with her father and several older siblings. They're middle class and have few resources for extras beyond the daily expenses of a large family.

Alexis found her way to her current school through an opportunity program for gifted students that her father learned about from a neighbor. Her older siblings have attended minority-majority public schools, with mixed results. While a couple of them have done reasonably well, none plan to attend college. One struggles in school and seems at high risk of dropping out.

Alexis loves her school. She appears to fit in well with her peer group, even though many of her classmates have very different identities and backgrounds from hers. Having been at the school for three years, she reports that she's acclimated well to the majority culture there. Her teachers and classmates would agree with that assessment.

At home and in her predominantly Black community, Alexis speaks in the way she learned to speak as a child, the way her family and her neighbors speak—using the same expressions, same grammar, same references, and same intonations. At school, Alexis switches her speech to match that of her mostly white classmates.

Though she says she changes the way she talks without even thinking about it, her mind still must work hard to make the shift whether she realizes it or not. Simply feeling the need to code-switch expends energy and causes tension in her body. She is always on and rarely fully relaxed.

At school, speaking like her white classmates, she's hiding her home-self to an extent. At home, when she forgets to make the switch, her siblings mock her and comment that she's "acting white." At a time in her life when she is defining who she is, Alexis must have to juggle different versions of herself, depending on where she is.

It would be optimal for Alexis to feel she didn't need to code-switch. But until then, what can relieve the stress is having a safe space to talk—in her authentic voice for her. In addition to our conversations, she has meaningful dialogue with a Black girls' affinity group at her school called "Sisters." Within this group, she feels can be herself completely. The handful of other students in Sisters relate to many aspects of Alexis's code-switching and other daily lived experiences. Thanks to this group, Alexis feels not only more connected and securely situated in the world, but more integrated within her developing self.

If you're a person of color, you're likely familiar with the concept of code-switching as you may well have lived it. The need to "code-switch" adds a heavy layer of stress for our students of color in white-majority schools—and more confusion for teachers trying to unpack the meanings and causes of stu-

dent behavior. Code-switching takes plac[e] behaviors and speech patterns based on with. Technically, code-switching refers languages when engaging with people language, language variety, or dialect fro

In white-majority and/or affluent sch switching tends to be common practice—o students who are non-white, non-affluent assimilation in a context where their sub style is not as powerful or even accepted don't feel they have any choice but to as though they may well hold onto their or "code" when they go home or interact friends from their neighborhoods.

To a certain extent, we all code-sw mary identities. We all have multiple a we express in different ways dependir you're in front of your classroom, you when you're at home on the couch six-year-old.

For students in settings where thei the dominant one, code-switching becc get along. But because their identities in their development, code-switching danger, more confusion, and more st adults who have a more stable identit[y]

What You Can Do at School

Every school can establish policies a positive racial and ethnic identities. lower student anxiety and mental he toward creating a school communit[y] from its diversity. Here are five such a

Supp

As A affin safe some come them cultu

S with out. may may

A tiated their divers

Encou

Ask t and st

Check

In my ences, writte the sa ture, a literatu tory to white reflect

By expanc and the

So, look over your curriculum. Are you aware of the vantage points of the authors of your textbook or primary sources? If you're teaching English, do your reading assignments represent authors with a range of racial and ethnic identities? Are they relatable for students from a range of personal backgrounds? If you're teaching history or psychology, is there a range of voices and diverse thoughts you can bring to the discussion? It's not that you can't include white male authors or Western perspectives, it's that you might consider naming them as such and adding other perspectives to balance things out.

I work with a student who immigrated from Colombia at age eleven and now attends a white-majority high school here in Boston. During one of our sessions, she was laughing about how "wrong" her history textbook was when it came to fundamental facts of South American history. To be honest, some of the issues she detailed came as a surprise to me. Now, these "facts" are disputable depending on one's country of origin, knowledge base, and cultural identity. (Case in point, some of the discrepancies she explained came as a surprise to me.) But think of the benefit to all the students in that Boston high school if they were to get the South American perspective on South American history along with the North American point of view.

A class that offers diverse sources creates a more interesting and truer learning experience for students. It teaches them to consider the limitations of their own lens, as well as the lens of the person who produced the source material. It teaches them the importance of seeking out a range of views. Those lessons alone will enrich their thinking and relationships for the rest of their lives.

Use Racial and Cultural Insensitivity as a Teaching Moment

When I present at professional development conferences, I start each session with this request, "If you have reason to take issue with something another participant says, please follow this motto: Cancel the idea, not the person."

Adolescents are learning about the world. Not only is their lens limited, but their lived experience and their empathy are as well. Thus, it should be no surprise when teenagers in the majority population are insensitive to their peers who are not. Most don't know any better. If they're expressing discriminatory ideas or ideologies, chances are they've gotten them from their parents, peer group, or social media. When similar transgressions happen in the classroom, it's not a moment for attacking and shaming. For your students, it's a moment for learning and growing. For you, it's a moment for remembering that their minds are developing, not developed. And there's real opportunity in that.

Approach educating students about issues of equity and inclusion just as you do your academic subject. Talk in general and not from a personal point of view—this is especially true if their words have been aimed at you. Frame the issue as the offending student's misunderstanding. Inform them that it's a misperception that "a lot of people have" (because they do).

Normalizing the student's misperception is important here, just as it would be if they couldn't grasp an equation or the theme of a short story. The goal here is not to humiliate them for their ignorance but to lead them toward knowledge, so they can better communicate about these complex societal issues.

Approach the Topic of Mental Health with Cultural Awareness

When making school policies and protocols around mental health care, remember to take into consideration cultural sensitivity about this subject. Not every culture embraces mental health care.

Should you have to talk with parents, remember that their context concerning mental health care may differ dramatically from your school's and your own. When I suggested to the anxious boy from a Nigerian family that his parents find him a psychologist, his response was, "Oh, that won't work. For Nigerian parents, mental health is not a thing." Similarly, a first-generation American student of Russian descent told me, "My parents don't believe in mental health." Of course, there are adults from every cultural background who are resistant to mental health care, but in some cultures, mental health really "is not a thing."

Several Asian-American students have explained to me that framing mental health issues in the language of the body and medicine can facilitate their parents' ability to follow up on a recommendation of professional support. It's a technique I've put to use with hesitant parents from a wide variety of backgrounds. I have found that families who wouldn't consider reaching out to a mental health professional may be willing to start with their pediatrician. And pediatricians are becoming, by necessity, more facile than ever before at managing mental health issues and making appropriate referrals for specialized care.

Teach the Whole Student

None of us are fully represented by a single aspect of our identity. And the same is true of our students. We teach best when we strive to see the whole student in context. We live best when we cultivate the simple awareness that everyone is coming at things from their own identity, their own perspective.

When we are sensitive to all the racial and cultural identities in our classrooms, we are better able to reach all our students. When we ensure our instruction is inclusive, we let our students know that all points of view—including theirs—are valid and worthy of study. When we make the effort to halt our bias and try to see a situation from our student's identity, we make better decisions about how to educate them and help them grow. It's not that we won't make mistakes, but by laying a foundation of recognition, curiosity, and respect, our students will be more emotionally robust, and any mistakes will be better tolerated and absorbed.

Diversity, equity, inclusion and belonging is a foundational component of student mental health and wellness.

Talk It Out: A Scenario and Questions for Discussion

Just as in previous chapters, read through the scenario below. Then answer the questions that follow yourself or with a group of colleagues.

You are a new teacher in racially diverse school. Looking to jump right into the community, you are chaperoning the first dance of the year for seventh and eighth graders. While on duty, you notice two of your female students in conversation with two male classmates. A few minutes later, you see the girls rush off to the bathroom together, leaving the boys behind. At that moment, a fellow chaperone strikes up a conversation with you, so you lose track of the situation.

On Monday morning, you are immediately reminded of the dance when you see one of the girls, Jennifer, in class. Generally, a cheerful, even buoyant, kid she is uncharacteristically quiet and looks dispirited. She lingers after the other students file out and you ask, "How did you like the dance on Friday?"

Looking like she's on the verge of tears, Jennifer tells you about the experience you inadvertently witnessed from afar. She tells you that she and her friend approached several White boys to ask them to dance. One of them said, "No, we don't want to dance with girls who look like you." Then the other boy nodded and laughed. She said she knew immediately what he meant, that he was referring to the fact that she and her friend are Black, while the boys are both white.

Jennifer discloses that this isn't the first time this sort of thing has happened at school.

Discussion Questions

1 What more would you want to learn if you found yourself in this situation? How might you obtain this information? Are there any barriers to gathering it?

2 Are there any action steps you'll consider? If so, what are they and why are you considering them? Are there any barriers to taking these steps?

3 Would you consider pulling a colleague at school into the loop? If so, who might you ask?
4 How do you believe you can best serve Jennifer's needs in this situation? What about her friend? And the boys?

Bibliography

1) Crenshaw, Kimberle. (1989) Demarginalizing the intersection of race and sex: A black feminist critique of antidiscrimination doctrine, feminist theory and antiracist politics. *University of Chicago Legal Forum.* https://chicagounbound.uchicago.edu/cgi/viewcontent.cgi?article=1052&context=uclf
2) Tatum, Beverly. (1997; Updated 2017) *Why Are All the Black Kids Sitting Together in the Cafeteria?* Basic Books.

6

Socioeconomic Considerations

I have many of the same stressors as my rich friends; mine have layers of pressure though, that most of my peers don't have to think about. I don't have the money or at times, the time to get some of the help that they do … so I smile a lot and just say things are okay.

– Twelfth grader

Generation Z students are coming of age at a time when the economic divide in the United States is more gaping than ever before. In the schools where I consult, there are numerous families with extreme wealth, whether it's intergenerational or earned through traditional avenues or the contemporary industries of financial services or technology. Students from these families travel between multiple homes and never need to think about the dramatically rising cost of things like college tuition. Meanwhile, some of their classmates come from families where essential expenses—including adequate housing, food, and medical care—are barely within reach.

DOI: 10.4324/9781003358923-8

Affluent, poor, or somewhere in the rapidly shrinking middle, the economic circumstances and level of privilege of a student's family color their experience of and reaction to the broader world. Of course, this is also true of adults—in workplaces, churches, town meetings. However, as in all aspects of identity, the effects are intense for adolescents.

To adolescents, socioeconomic circumstances are another piece of the complex identity puzzle they're working to piece together. Adolescents use their family's socioeconomic status— for better and worse—to gauge who they are, where they and their families or communities fit, and how they measure up against their peers.

Understanding that socioeconomic disparities can create tensions among students, some schools take steps to "level the playing field" on campus. Some schools require uniforms, for example, in an attempt to eliminate class differentiation. (Though some argue uniforms do more harm than good in that they quash a teenager's natural drive to explore and express their identity and individuality through clothing choices.)

In a similar effort, several school counselors I know who practice in private schools encourage both faculty and students not to ask where others "went" on spring break. In affluent and even middle-class communities, many students routinely take expensive family trips—to tropical islands, Europe, and elsewhere. But some students do not because their families can't afford such trips. So, the question becomes an assumption and expectation that can leave those in the latter category uncomfortable, embarrassed, and even more left out.

To "level the playing field" in this area, the counselors suggest asking different kinds of questions: "Did you see any good movies over break?" "Did you catch up on sleep?" While this doesn't resolve the equity gap, the counselors feel it protects students who don't travel at every school vacation from feeling even worse about it.

In my own work in schools, I've heard from numerous students from middle- and lower-income households, that holiday breaks actually can be quite difficult. Not necessarily because their families can't take fancy vacations, but because after the first couple of days binge-watching TV, there simply isn't that much to do. Their parents work, so the students are left without a ride to friends' houses or, in the case of older students, a car to borrow. And without much expendable cash, these students can't easily while away their time shopping or go to amusement parks. Numerous students have told me that, while they initially enjoy the break from homework, they miss the structure, connection, and activity that school provides.

If you work in a school with a range of family income levels and material privilege you likely witness social-class dynamics and tensions play out in more ways than just clothes and vacations. In order to understand how social-class differences among our students affect their relationships with each other—and with us—we must consider how socio-economic status affects our students' view of themselves within the broader social context.

Money and Parenting

In her comprehensive, landmark study, *Unequal Childhoods: Class, Race, and Family Life*, University of Pennsylvania sociologist Annette Lareau found that the biggest differences in child rearing styles in the United State were not necessarily between Black and white families but across socioeconomic classes. She writes, "It is in these class differences and how they are enacted in family life and child rearing that shape the ways children view themselves in relation to the rest of the world." She distinguishes between two models of child rearing: "concerted cultivation" and "natural growth."

Middle-class parents tend toward concerted cultivation in their parenting. In this model, most of a child's time is structured in specific activities. They are often supervised by a parent, coach, or counselor. Their goals and desires are freely discussed and facilitated. Thus, these children become comfortable speaking to adults and making requests of them to get their needs met.

In the natural growth model—which is more often the model of working-class and lower-income parents—children structure their own time and activities. They interact mostly with their peers and learn to solve problems within that group. They rarely engage in conversation with adults outside their family. Thus, they tend to be more deferential to adults they don't know. This often makes them better mannered and more polite than children from affluent homes. But it also makes them reluctant to speak up when they need something.

Concerted cultivation is generally in line with how schools work, not to mention with the assumptions educators, pediatricians, and mental health professionals tend to have about how children should work. (All of us are highly educated, and some of us are from middle- or upper-class families, where we were ourselves raised via concerted cultivation.) To children from concerted-cultivation upbringings, the classroom is familiar territory. They know the rules. They speak the language. So, it's no wonder they tend to have an easier time succeeding academically and socially in school.

While there is much to tout about the benefits of natural growth, to a child raised in this model, school can be a foreign land. Their life experience is out of sync with what goes on in school. Suddenly, their time is structured. The rules aren't worked out among peers but come down from on high—with the reasoning behind them seldom explained. Because of their natural reluctance to approach an adult or "take up their time," they don't receive the guidance or academic help they might need. Essentially, natural-growth children are left to pick up on all the innuendos of school culture on their own. And eventually, this unpreparedness causes struggles, tensions, and misunderstandings, which can turn into a lifelong "distrust" of institutions and authority figures themselves.

Just having an awareness of these differences can change the way you relate and respond to your students. It can provide insight as to how a particular student might be processing a situation or what they might need from you.

One student from a poor family commented to me about her experience visiting the New England boarding school she'd been accepted to. "All the students are so enthusiastic and talkative, especially around teachers," she said. She wondered whether she needed to work on her "social skills" before starting high school there.

This was a gracious, warm, friendly girl whose "social skills" seemed more than solid to me. I acknowledged that I could see how she might not yet feel comfortable talking to adults in the casual way she talks with middle-school classmates or even with adults she knows well, like me. I suggested that once she's there, she'll learn to feel more comfortable chatting with adults the way she saw the other kids doing.

Intersectionality and Interaction

Just as we did when considering race and culture, we can consider intersectionality from a socioeconomic point of view in our relationships with students. Often teachers come from different socioeconomic backgrounds than their students. If you're a teacher with a working-class upbringing, for example, who's teaching students like those my patient encountered at the New England boarding school, you may find those students' attitudes surprising, even off-putting. On the other hand, if you're a boarding school graduate from a middle- or upper-class background, it may not be intuitive to you that the non-solicitous or even "passive" nature of certain students may be reflecting their class background as much as their personalities.

It's not that being quiet around teachers is necessarily detrimental, and it's hard to tell with adolescents whether they are simply so kid-centric that they don't think to strike up a conversation with teachers. But where we need to pay attention is when a student from a less-privileged background needs help and isn't asking for it. This is an opportunity for us to step in and make it easy for them to reach out to us, so they don't miss out.

It's useful for us to think about how our own social-class identity—both current and historical—affects our views and biases, and so our relationships with and expectations of our students. We need to recognize that our social-class identity contributes to our strengths as educators, as well as our limitations and blind spots.

While teaching a college course on human development, my students asked me whether marrying earlier or later is optimal from the point of view of adult development and family. I instinctively began to spout off my answer (the later the better, and here's why …) and then stopped myself, recognizing the bias in my first thought had been created by my own socioeconomic background. So I took the opportunity not to talk about the optimal marriage age—because really, what would that be and who's to say—but to speak about how our personal biases can lead us to opinions or conclusions that reflect not a definitive reality but our individual background and lived experience. It's not that my answer was "wrong," but it was far from objective.

Of course, it's easier to stop mid-lecture and take such a tangent with college students. Their abstract thinking and capacity for empathy (including to their instructor's missteps) is stronger than those of many high-school—and surely, middle-school—students. Still, this was a reminder to me, and a relatively benign example for you, of how we—as the adults in the room with deep, complex histories and formed identities, as well as authority—can and must "step back" when necessary to consider the points of view of our students and their families. We must learn to pause our thoughts and ask ourselves, "Am I bringing my own values or assumptions to my assessment of this situation? Are they getting in the way of my fully understanding the problem and the best options for how to address it?"

Cultivating Economic Sensitivity

As with race and culture, socioeconomic status is more salient for students who are in the non-majority group. The makeup of your particular school community determines the details here. As students enter middle school and into high school, socioeconomic differences become more pronounced. While these differences show up in what they wear, drive, and where they go on vacation, more alarming and consequential is that they begin to show up in the opportunities students have. At this age, a very real opportunity gap—for enriching summer experiences, substantive job-shadowing, or internship opportunities—becomes more apparent.

Activities and opportunities that many of their peers take for granted are simply off-limits to students from poorer families. After all, it costs money to do things, to participate, and to take advantage of opportunities such as special field trips, unpaid internships, high-school sports, or even getting pizza with friends after school. Emotionally, this can set poorer students up for hurt or insult. For practical reasons, they find themselves having to duck out of activities with friends because they can't afford them.

On the other hand, those in the majority socioeconomic class are set up for insensitivity—especially when the majority is wealthy or upper middle class. Not always conscious of their privilege because they've never known anything else, these students may have misperceptions about socioeconomic conditions different from their own. Those misperceptions are drawn from the usual sources—popular culture (news, media, entertainment platforms), parental opinions, and their peers.

Ella, a seventh grader at an affluent independent school, was hanging out with a group of friends when one of the girls commented, "Our school should not be wasting money on financial aid … There are a lot of other things they could be spending that money on." The girl didn't know Ella was receiving substantial financial aid, without which she would never be able to attend their school.

Though Ella didn't feel comfortable speaking up at that moment, the "in-her-head" response she voiced to me later was not only clear and direct, but deeper and more far-reaching than she knew: "Does she think education is just for rich people?"

While many (though by no means all) Gen Z students are relatively thoughtful and sensitive about racial-ethnic differences among their peers, fewer may be aware of the delicate, possibly painful, nature of social-class disparities. And these issues are hard for adults to talk about. Cultivating sensitivity to the differences does not fall into a specific or easily identifiable domain. Yet, if there are significant disparities or even a substantial range within a school community, it's an important subject to address—not just for students but for us as faculty members, too.

I consulted with an eleventh grader named Beatriz, who'd suffered an episode of anxiety so extreme she was hospitalized for several days. Beatriz was a low-income student who had immigrated to the U.S. from South America with her family just a few years before. She was at a predominately white boarding school where, she told me, she'd never felt comfortable at school and her anxiety had been building for some time.

Beatriz had always done well academically, never requiring any special support or attention. Her response to the social stress she was feeling was to hold her feelings in. She didn't tell her mother, her teachers, or her friends how she was feeling. Finally, she "snapped," becoming so panicked, even disoriented, that her mother took her to the emergency room.

Once discharged from a brief psychiatric hospital stay with prescriptions for medication and individual counseling with me, Beatriz was more stable but extremely apprehensive about of re-entering the same school environment, with the same workload that she felt had driven her to the brink. Because Beatriz looked fine, her teachers and the school never thought to alter her academic demands when she returned. And Beatriz didn't ask.

Beatriz's mother, though deeply concerned about her daughter's stress level, did not ask either. She knew her daughter was overwhelmed by academic demands and struggling within a social context where she felt she didn't "fit." But her mother didn't speak English and wasn't confident, even with a translator, to ask for more support for her daughter. She felt the school had already given Beatriz so much and the family shouldn't ask for anything "extra."

So, I reached out to the upper-school head to discuss what might be done to alleviate some of Beatriz's stress. I let her know that Beatriz was not doing as well as she looked and that she was still extremely anxious. I explained that Beatriz was unable to reveal her distress to her teachers or academic advisor because she was afraid of disappointing them. She also felt grateful for the comprehensive financial-aid package she was receiving and did not feel comfortable requesting anything further from the school. This particular administrator (who in the course of conversation, let me know she herself had been a low-income scholarship student in an independent school) rallied Beatriz's teachers. Together, they enacted a workload reduction.

Though she still felt like an outsider and was somewhat isolated socially at school, once Beatriz felt better, she joined a local Saturday program in her neighborhood for youth entrepreneurship. In this group, she was with students who looked like her, shared many of her life experiences, and came from the same socioeconomic background. Even though Beatriz never came to feel fully at home with her classmates, she found a way to continue her educational path while drawing on the entrepreneurship group to meet her identity and social-emotional needs.

To have a healthy school community and give all our students the opportunities they deserve, we need to do all we can to ensure inclusion and prevent exclusion due to a student's socioeconomic circumstances. In a school setting where the majority of students can participate in whatever they want without thinking about finances, we need to be sensitive to those students who cannot and find ways to identify, and even generate, resources for them. These can be school-based opportunities, access to programs with scholarships or stipends, or a fund that provides need-based allocations for opportunities important to their education and for feeling included in school life.

Too Much of a Good Thing

Beatriz's story shows that when we take the time to understand our students more fully, we can respond in meaningful and beneficial ways. As we work toward inclusion, we need to check our bias when it comes to students from advantaged backgrounds as well.

While it can be hard to maintain empathy for an extremely privileged student, especially one who flaunts their family's wealth, we need to open our minds to the fact that their perspective of the world and what's possible for them can be just as skewed (if not more so, because their situation is praised and viewed by the greater world as fortunate) as someone's from a lower-class background. Just because a kid comes from an economically stable household and has been raised in the concerted-cultivation model doesn't mean they don't face hurdles on their way to maturity.

Recent research by psychologist Suniya Luthar reveals what she terms "the price of privilege." Luthar began studying mental health issues in economically disadvantaged students, using affluent students as a "control" or comparison group. But what she soon found was affluent adolescents were somewhat more likely to suffer from mental health issues than their less privileged peers. Within her robust body of empirical literature about the strain on affluent students in high-achieving schools, Luthar documents several factors that contribute to these students' distress, including parents who may expect "perfection," a personal tendency toward perfection, and persistent envy of peers.

Luthar found an association between neighborhood affluence and high delinquency. While lower-income, inner-city teens were participating in crimes of self-defense and destitution (such as carrying a weapon, selling drugs, or stealing something they couldn't afford), their affluent, suburban counterparts were stealing from their parents or friends for the thrill of it, cheating on tests, or taking illegal drugs (which their money allowed them to afford). In addition, suburban kids suffered from higher rates of depression, anxiety, and somatic symptoms than the national norm. And sadly, she found, these issues followed them to college. (Luthar, 2013)

Even when alarming issues such as drugs, delinquency, or depression aren't present, being raised with money can still cause suffering in adolescents trying to individuate and figure out who they are beyond their parents' privilege.

Jake, a boy referred to my practice by his elite, independent high school, came from an extremely affluent family. As he would be the first to tell you. He often drove himself to his appointment in a car that looked like it may have cost—just a guesstimate—more than my office.

In our sessions, Jake talked proudly about his father, who he (accurately) described as a "self-made man." Jake glowed with admiration for his father's accomplishments and the luxuries their wealth provided. Barely underneath the surface, I observed Jake's wistfulness and longing for his father's affection and approval. The message he'd received from his homelife was that those things—like all things—were to be earned, and he was unsure how to do that. Jake also confided that it was hard to find close, reliable friends. He worried that people only liked him for his money. Interestingly, I observed it was Jake who kept the topic of his money front and center in our sessions.

When I spoke with Jake's school counselor, he mentioned that Jake sometimes behaved in ways that turned other kids off. For example, on a school field trip, Jake far outspent his peers in visible ways. The counselor suspected it was Jake's way of trying to win approval and elevate his status, but he and I agreed that, of course, it did just the opposite. While it was a clear material advantage, Jake's family's wealth had become a barrier to the love and friendship he urgently wanted in his life.

About a year into my work with Jake, he found a new girl-friend. As he described how comfortable he felt with her, he mentioned that she was from a family who owned a well-known, multinational company. It turned out that Jake's girlfriend also worried that other kids were interested in her more for her family's wealth and prominence than for herself. This commonality, I realized, wasn't only a bond between Jake and his girlfriend. To him, their shared economic status felt like built-in reassurance that she wasn't using him.

I don't know how this romance—or Jake, for that matter—turned out in the long run because a few months after falling head-over-heels for this girl, Jake decided he no longer needed therapy. He announced that the anxieties and insecurities that had brought him to my office had subsided, and he was finally happy.

Socioeconomics and Mental Health

Again, just as with racial and cultural identities, people from different socioeconomic classes often have different opinions of and familiarity with mental health care. We need to be consid-erate of this when speaking to families about their children's emotional or behavioral problems in school or their mental health directly.

When privileged parents contact me in my practice, most are casual and comfortable talking with me over the phone. Their conversational style conveys to me a level of ease derived from privilege. I'm a resource which they feel safe drawing on. They treat me more as a peer than an authority figure. I am one of many resources at their disposal—along with writing tutors, col-lege consultants, and tennis coaches—to support their child.

But for parents who are neither affluent nor highly educated, nor from a culture or community where seeking mental health care is a common event, our initial conversations are often more formal. Many such parents sound careful, polite, even hesitant to take up my time.

You may have had comparable experiences with parents in your school community. Do they treat you as a partner? Or an expert? Or does it seem like you are their employee? Or do you feel like they see you as a potentially intimidating authority figure?

Even when mental health issues don't carry stigma in a family, the economic barriers to mental health care discourage anyone with a tight budget. Therapy is expensive and insurance often limits access to providers and the extent of covered services. Adding to these difficulties, there's a dearth of child-adolescent mental health providers. Community mental health centers or hospital-based clinics typically have exceedingly long waiting lists, as well.

To counter these costs and get low-income students the care they need, many school counselors reserve a few slots in their schedule for appointments. This need not be a formal or official arrangement. Most school counselors I know have done this as the need has presented itself, organically. It is important, however, to account for the way this time is spent when discussing budgets and professional responsibilities with school administration and leadership.

What You and Your School Can Do

In addition to your school counselor agreeing to take on a few students as regulars, there are several other things you and your school community can do to ensure a student's socioeconomic circumstances and their identity with it doesn't limit them as a student or a person.

Take Advantage of Teaching Moments

When you encounter socioeconomic insensitivity or ignorance in your students or in your course work, use it as an opportunity to expand your students' thinking around socioeconomic issues, being careful not to call out or embarrass any one student. This is also an opportunity to encourage their emerging capacity for empathy.

Examine Your Own Bias

Remember Jake? At one point, he told me he thought his history teacher didn't like him. I suspected Jake might be right. Jake could sound and act pretty obnoxious about his family's wealth. And he let me know that he had a sticker on his computer supporting a political candidate with views that favored wealthy Americans over all others. Jake suspected his history teacher might be judging him for the sticker. Again, I figured I could trust Jake's gut on this one.

However, my job—and yours—is to pause our bias or automatic thoughts and understand where all our students (even the Jakes among them) are coming from, and how their socioeconomic circumstances might inform their thinking and behavior.

When I was mindful and clear about my own bias, I could look past the wealth-flaunting to see that Jake was a vulnerable sixteen-year-old, desperate to belong and be accepted—not just at school but within his own family. Because I had the luxury of time, space, and conversation, it didn't take me long to recognize that Jake's parents were materially indulgent but largely emotionally unavailable to him.

Every behavior comes from somewhere. As educators, we need to figure out what that "somewhere" looks like for each of our students. With my bias out of the way and my own empathy for Jake forged, I was able to help him work on his empathy for other people in the time we had together.

Inquire Before Accusing

With your bias on pause, use your open mind to also consider the real issues behind a student's late paper, sleeping in class, or not studying for a test. Before you accuse them of being lazy or distracted (both normal behaviors for teens, by the way), inquire what happened, what caused them not to follow through the way you expected them to—and consider the possibility of socioeconomic demands.

Even when education is highly prioritized in their home, teenagers from lower-income households often have responsibilities beyond school. That late paper or failed test could be the result of your student having to stay late at their after-school job or care for a sick sibling while their parents worked a night shift.

Make it your policy to ask first. And then work with them to get them beyond their hurdles so they can have the education they need.

Create a Parent Affinity Group

If you teach in an independent school that serves primarily affluent families, consider an affinity group for parents who are not affluent. It's one of the easiest and best ways to make families who are not from the majority socioeconomic status feel like they're not alone, they're supported, and they are being listened to. At one Boston-area school, the family engagement coordinator started a group called "First Generation Parents' Group" for those families who were engaging with an independent school for the first time.

Educate Yourself About College Scholarships/Financial Aid for Lower-income Students

If you're part of your high school's college advising program, consider expanding your office's knowledge of financial aid and scholarship programs. The result will expand opportunities for students from low-income families and improve their chances of attending their first-choice institutions.

Closing the Wealth Gap

When it comes to socioeconomics, we can't completely level the playing field for our students—that just won't happen. But when we take the time to notice where our students are positioned on that field, learn how they got there, and consider the obstacles they're likely to face because of it, we as educators are better positioned ourselves to help them manage those obstacles and get to the finish line of their choosing. Maybe even get them there with a greater understanding of and empathy for people, no matter their tax bracket.

Talk It Out: A Scenario and Questions for Discussion

Read through the scenario below. Then answer the questions that follow yourself or with a group of colleagues.

Jordan, a tenth grader in your advisory who was somewhat reserved and "business-like" last year has begun to confide in you about some of the social stresses he experiences at school. He mentions, with hesitation, that it's been difficult to adapt to a school community full of students who can afford to go out for lunch virtually every day. He says that most of his peers assume it's no big deal. But to him, spending ten dollars on a meal is totally out of the question. He adds that other kids will offer to pay for him. But he knows he can't pay them back and so declines. Not to mention that once, last year, he ventured to accept his friend's offer to pay for him, and then some of them joked about it later in a way that made him feel self-conscious and uncomfortable.

He confides that this all feels awkward, and he does not mean to complain, but he's not sure how to explain his situation to his friends in such a way that they'll stop asking, not take it personally—and most of all, not feel sorry for him.

Discussion Questions

1 Is Jordan's situation familiar to you, or does it come as a surprise?
2 How do you think this situation looks and feels from Jordan's point of view?
3 Is there more you want to learn from Jordan, about this predicament? About any other aspects of his experience at school? Is there anything you want to tell him?
4 What have you seen about how social class differences play out within your school community, in this way or others?
5 Is there anything you, or your school, does to acknowledge or address social class disparities among students and families?

Bibliography

1) Lareau, Annette. (2011) *Unequal Childhoods: Class, Race and Family Life*. 2nd edition with an Update a Decade Later. University of California Press.
2) Luthar, Suniya. (2013) I can, therefore I must: Fragility in the upper-middle class. *Development and Psychopathology*, 25th Anniversary Special Issue, 25: 1529–1549.

7

Gender Identity and Sexual Orientation

LGBTQ+ youth are not inherently prone to suicide risk because of their sexual orientation or gender identity, but rather they are placed at higher risk because of how they are mistreated and stigmatized in society.

– The Trevor Project

Euphoria, the HBO series of record-breaking popularity, features seventeen-year-old Rue Bennett, a non-binary lesbian, who is also biracial (born to one Black and one white parent), as the main character. Rue's struggles with drug abuse and mental health issues (bipolar disorder, anxiety, and ADHD) make their life more dramatic, complex, and nuanced to the delight of the audience.

The series is "intended" for viewers seventeen years and older, but I hear about many students as young as eighth grade being major fans. We can debate whether the show's content is appropriate for those younger kids. But no matter how well we argue, the reality will still be that Gen Z middle schoolers and

DOI: 10.4324/9781003358923-9

high schoolers alike are going to watch the show. They do so because Rue's character encompasses many of the issues and identities that their generation is curious about and working to understand in themselves, their friends, and in the larger society.

As we all know too well, middle- and secondary-school students are (or will soon be) in a biological stage called puberty that corresponds to gender- and sexuality-specific changes. As their bodies transform and their hormones flow, they're trying to figure out what these changes mean to who they are and who they are becoming, both gender-wise and sexually.

At the same time, American culture is pouncing on adolescents' emerging selves with countless pressures, expectations, and biases of its own in this fraught and intensely personal area of identity. Today's students might enjoy more choice and more acceptance among peers for whatever their preferences turn out to be, but with more choice often comes confusion. Imagine yourself at thirteen or fifteen or even eighteen trying to understand and navigate—the possibilities that our students are weighing today. Imagine the huge task of figuring out—maybe on your own—what each sexual orientation or gender identity is, what it means to adopt it, and what feels right.

The Generational Divide

When I was growing up in the 1970s, a girl one grade ahead of me in elementary school, Sue, looked and acted more "like a boy" than the other girls I knew. She had very short hair, though at that time long hair was the dominant fashion for girls and women. Her physical build was "stocky," her voice deep. She also tended to befriend boys rather than girls, which is not typical at that age. Kids did comment that Sue seemed "like a boy," though I don't recall the tone being critical or disparaging, but more matter of fact.

What sticks with me most about Sue, however, is while I stewed in relative silence over not being allowed to join the local Little League team—no girls allowed—Sue played on the team. I don't know what her parents said or how this was negotiated, but she was on the roster. And she was really good. I can still remember watching her in admiration, while also puzzling over how "different" she seemed. To Sue's and her parent's great credit, even in those times, Sue didn't allow a gender norm to stop her from pursuing her passions. I, on the other hand, identified wholly as a girl and did allow the social constructs of that identity to limit me.

Though I didn't know Sue well and certainly never discussed anything about gender with her (I'm sure we didn't even know that word), in retrospect, I wonder whether today Sue might have described her identity as non-binary, or transgender, or gender fluid. Maybe, maybe not. But, of course, neither Sue nor I nor anyone in our generation was offered such choices or knew they existed. All we could be, as we began to define our own identities, was male or female, straight or gay.

Over the past twenty-five years, working in schools in predominantly liberal communities, I've witnessed the shift in how middle- and high-school students conceive of and express sexual orientation and gender identity. In the early years of my career, there was one transgender student at the high school where I worked, and I had a single such teenager in my private practice. Only a few girls—and even fewer boys—were talking about identifying as bisexual.

In addition, though I likely had many LGBTQIA2S+ colleagues, the subject of sexuality was never broached in the faculty lounge. For the most part, heterosexuality was assumed. However, at one progressive secondary school where I worked in the early 2000s, a young teacher, who had long felt she was in the wrong body and wrongly categorized as female, did transition to a male identity.

At that time, transgender identity was just beginning to be recognized more broadly. So, when this teacher announced to the head of school that she was transitioning, she naturally worried about losing her job, which didn't happen. We faculty members wondered about what our students' reactions would be. It turns out, we should have worried more about our own. As the teacher's appearance changed along with his pronouns, it was we Baby Boomers and Gen X-ers who stumbled to adjust, despite the best of intentions. The students weren't phased in the least. They went from Ms. to Mr. without missing a beat.

Today, in the high schools I visit and in my counseling practice, many kids are identifying as gay, lesbian, or bisexual. It's no longer uncommon—for girls especially—to experiment with both male and female partners. Students as young as sixth and seventh grade speak to me of shifting gender identities (such as transgender, non-binary, and gender-fluid identities), something I once only heard rarely from older high-school or college students. And most recently, a couple of girls I work with, who by all appearances and conversations seem squarely in the female realm of identity, informed me they preferred to use "they/them" pronouns. One of them told me matter-of-factly, "I don't want to be constrained by people's ideas about how girls are supposed to be."

The Pew Research study, *On the Cusp of Adulthood and Facing an Uncertain Future: What We Know About Generation Z So Far* (2020), reports that Gen Z-ers are more likely to know someone using gender-neutral pronouns than those of us in previous generations. They're also more likely to think standard forms should offer gender options other than "man" and "woman."

In their 2016 book, *Generation Z Goes to College*, Corey Seemiller and Meghan Grace refer to Generation Z as "the gender bending generation." They accurately point out that this generation has only known a multi-faceted world where gender is concerned. Transgender celebrities like Caitlyn Jenner, gender-neutral bathrooms, and gender-inclusive language have been a normal presence in their world since their childhood. Based on all this, Seemiller and Grace predict, "Generation Z's open views on gender" will make issues of gender identity "front and center in discussions around policies and practices" as they move into adulthood. We certainly see evidence of this in our schools today.

There have already been seismic shifts in the way our society regards sex and gender. According to a Gallup poll, only 4.2 percent of Generation X (born between 1965 and 1980) and 10.5 percent of Millennials (born between 1981 and 1996) identify as LGBT, as compared with nearly 21 percent of Gen Z-ers. The generation gap is real when it comes to ideas on sex and gender.

While having choice, increased acceptance, and role models of every sexual orientation and gender identity, eliminates some problems for today's youth, we need to be aware that it may also create others. The ground in these sensitive areas continues to shift under our feet and theirs. Like race, ethnicity, and social class, sexual orientation and gender are factors in the identity the adolescent is creating for themselves. If we want to remain effective in the classroom and support our teenage students, it's imperative that we come to understand how this generation— and our individual students—view these issues.

A Few Definitions

Because vocabulary around sexual and gender identity is growing and changing as quickly as the culture itself, it might be helpful to nail down a few definitions before we go any further. I must add a disclaimer here: There are many different definitions of these terms. We must remain conscious that they refer to living, breathing issues and, as such, are evolving as we speak. Because it's difficult to capture a perfect or comprehensive denotation in a given moment, let's consider the following guidelines for thinking about these issues and identities:

- ◆ Sex – This word refers to the biological and physiological characteristics present at birth. These include chromosomal, hormonal, and anatomical differences between boys and girls.
- ◆ Gender – Gender is a social construct. It encompasses the social categories that are not purely a product of biology but rather the product of cultural beliefs and practices about how individuals in a category (traditionally, male or female) are expected to look and behave. These would include dress, occupation, likes, and dislikes, etc.
- ◆ Sexual orientation – This phrase refers to a pattern of emotional, romantic, and/or sexual attraction to other people. Examples include heterosexual, bisexual, gay, lesbian, and queer, among others.
- ◆ Gender identity – Gender identity denotes a person's feelings and experience of their own identification with a particular gender. Gender identity is not the same as sexual orientation, nor does it map directly to it in any specific way. Gender identities include cisgendered, transgendered, and non-binary, among others (all defined below). Gender identity is the reason many adolescents— and more recently, adults—specify their gender pronouns.
- ◆ Transgender – This term denotes or relates to a person whose sense of personal identity and gender does not correspond with their birth sex. Transgender students typically prefer to be known by the name they choose and by the pronouns of the gender they identify with (e.g., he, she, they).
- ◆ Non-binary – Non-binary individuals don't feel completely male or female. Instead, they feel a mix of the two or something different from either, on a separate plane or continuum. Non-binary individuals choose the

pronouns "they/them" because they feel these better describe who they are.

- Cisgender (or cis) – This term describes a person whose gender identity corresponds directly to their birth sex (e.g., a person born with male genitalia who identifies as a boy or a man).
- Bisexual – Someone who is bisexual is emotionally and sexually attracted to more than one gender, typically both men and women.
- Pansexual – A person who describes themselves as pansexual is emotionally and sexually attracted to all genders.
- Queer – This term is the vernacular for someone who identifies as an individual and as part of a broader community that rejects traditional categories of gender and sexuality. While the word "queer" was a slur used to describe gay people, today it has been reclaimed and repurposed by the community it describes.
- Intersex – Intersex individuals have reproductive anatomy or chromosomal characteristics that do not clearly fall into the biological category of male or female. This condition is present at birth.
- Asexual – An asexual person doesn't feel sexual attraction or feels it in a different or less intense way than the majority of the population.
- Two-spirit – This is a third gender described by traditional Native American cultures. A two-spirited person is neither a man nor a woman, but combines the activities, roles, and spirit of both men and women. While this description belongs to indigenous people and their cultures, it has been adopted by some non-native people, as well as co-opted by some queer-affirming groups and added to their acronym (below).
- LGBTQIA2S+ – This acronym stands for: lesbian, gay, bisexual, transgender, queer and/or questioning,

intersex, asexual, two-spirit, and any other affirmative way in which people choose to self-identify.

♦ Gender nonconforming – This term describes a person whose appearance and behavior do not conform to the social norms associated with their birth sex, e.g., a boy with long hair or painted fingernails; or a girl with very short hair or traditionally "masculine" clothes. This term does not connote sexual orientation.

♦ Gender fluid – Gender fluid is a state where a person's gender identity and expression change over time. Perhaps the identity moves back and forth between male and female, or to non-binary, not landing in either the male or the female category. For some adolescents, gender fluidity may be a way to explore gender before landing on a more unified gender expression or identity. It's important to know that not all kids who are gender fluid in adolescence will remain that way as adults. For others, gender fluidity may continue indefinitely and remain a central part of who they are.

The Danger Zone

As we all know, the biological stage called puberty corresponds to specific and very personal changes. Our students' body shapes are transforming before their eyes. Their hormones are intense. In the midst of all this physical and emotional tumult—or perhaps because of it—adolescents become desperate to know who they are and where, and if, they belong anywhere.

The other traits they are using to define themselves—racial, ethnic, and socio-economic circumstances—tie them to their families and communities of origin. They have been living with these traits their entire lives. They are known aspects, even though they are now seen by the teenager in a different, developmentally defined light.

While an adolescent might have to wrestle with these factors that have formed them and find new ways to integrate them into who they see themselves becoming, no part of our culture suggests that racial, ethnic, or socio-economic circumstances are "a choice" the adolescent makes or that they are within their control to change. While plenty of problems arise for the adolescent in coming to terms with these aspects of their identity, claiming these factors as part of who they are doesn't risk estrangement from their families or home communities.

This is not true for emerging sexual and gender identities. There is real danger here for our students. First, so much about sexuality and gender is new to them—for many it's not a topic discussed in their home. They don't know how to think about it and might not be sure of what's happening to them.

Second, as they're trying to understand their new bodies, new feelings, and new thoughts and desires, they're also responding to family and peer expectations, deep-seated cultural biases, not to mention marketing messages bombarding them with dictates to look this way, be this way, and feel like this. Multiplying the pressure, simply "trying on" a sexual or gender identity that goes against an expectation can put them in danger of being ostracized or physically harmed.

Thus, such major aspects of adolescent identity as sexuality and gender are danger zones—risk factors for social marginalization, mental health problems, and even suicide, especially in LGBTQIA2S+ youth. The rigid demarcations along gender lines that American society has rather miraculously maintained does little to benefit our students' emotional health. Between power dynamics and cultural pressure to conform to gendered expectations of both behavior and inner life, today's social norms tend to push girls to hold feelings in (resulting in anxiety and depression) and boys to act aggressively (resulting in harmful behavior to others, and many times to themselves as well).

As we've discussed, Generation Z students are markedly more likely than any other generation before them to identify as "queer"—along the dimension of sexual orientation, or gender identity, or both. The mental health vulnerabilities and risks to this sub-population of students has long been documented as dramatically higher than that of any other sub-population, making these students prone to anxiety, depression, and thoughts and acts of self-harm, including suicide. In addition, students with non-heterosexual, gender nonconforming identities are also more likely to be marginalized or targeted for exclusion, bullying, and violence.

Puberty and emerging sexuality are exciting, but they are also a time of agitation, stress, and upset. Here are the major stressors all our students—but especially our LGBTQIA2S+ students—are facing during this period of development and identity formation:

Confusion

When it comes to issues of sexuality and gender identity, many adolescents are struggling and confused about this new, complex territory. They may have questions, doubts, fears, and insecurities. For LGBTQIA2S+ students, these feelings may be even more intense.

Insensitivity and Bullying

At this age, peer norms are being established, and kids who go against them can suffer mightily. Middle- and high-school students often say things that are harmful without really intending to. For instance, for all the enlightenment Gen Z demonstrates around issues of sexuality and gender, I'm sure you've heard the term "gay" used as a pejorative by your students.

But while words can hurt and do significant damage on their own, LGBTQIA2S+ students often must also deal with threats to their physical safety. All bullying is a reaction—usually born out of fear that any difference presents—but understanding that doesn't eliminate the very real danger that LGBTQIA2S+ students, or any students who don't conform to social norms, must navigate.

The Home Front: Parent-child Relationship

Even when the parent-child relationship is otherwise harmonious, the child's search for identity vis-a-vis sexual orientation or gender can cause conflict or distance. This is especially so when the adolescent's search leads them to an identity that conflicts with their parents' values. In this case, the adolescent may feel or fear they've lost a major support in their life. They may feel especially adrift, having lost that all-important sense of belonging.

Suicide

According to the Trevor Project's National Survey on LGBTQ+ Youth Mental Health 2021, 42 percent of LGBTQ+ youth considered suicide in 2021. Half of them identified as transgender or non-binary. All the pressures and perils we address above feed into these percentages. The result is that students identifying as LGBTQIA2S+ are at markedly higher risk of suicide than that of any other distinct adolescent identity group.

Your School Has an Identity, Too

As a school community—and individual educators—we have a choice: We can add to the pressures and risks our students face as they come to terms with their emerging sexuality, or we can be a place of acceptance, where students can learn to understand themselves and their peers and where they can search for whoever they are without fear of bullying or expulsion. School can be a place of refuge and understanding, a lifeline for students who find themselves shunned by their family, church, or home community during this confusing time. A school community can be a place where at-risk populations are an increasingly visible, vibrant, and active part of the student population.

Recently, at a professional development conference for school administrators—many of whom were from church-affiliated schools—I presented a scenario about a student who was questioning and exploring their gender identity. This student was also displaying enough anxiety that a school might need to consider looping the parents in. One of my questions to the attendees was: How does your school policy inform the response of the school counselor and dean of students in such a case?

The answers represented a wide spectrum of what students find when they turn to their school for help. On one end, a representative from a Unitarian Universalist school said, "… all identities are accepted and supported. We would work with the student to make sure they feel recognized and included, and with the parents to help them support their child." On the other end, the administrator from a school identifying itself as Christian, said, "… we believe that gender is assigned at birth by the Lord. If a student is questioning that, we would refer the family to our handbook. Ours may not be the right school for their child."

As the above comments illustrate, some environments are not only inclusive but explicitly supportive of LGBTQIA2S+ students, while others exclude them as a matter of policy. Most schools, likely yours, fall somewhere in the middle of that continuum—with "middle" reflecting not so much as part way or between, but rather a mix or collection of policies, practices, and behaviors.

For example, your school as an institution may be inclusive and respectful of all sexual orientations and gender identities. But some students may make disparaging comments about their peers and go uncorrected. Or some parents or teachers may not be familiar or comfortable with the gender fluidity of Generation Z.

While a lack of familiarity and comfort on the part of older generations may be as understandable and explainable as the ignorance and lack of empathy from peers, if your school's intention is to be an inclusive, respectful environment, you must ask whether the adults and students in the school community can grasp enough of the basics to ensure that students with a full range of sexual orientations and gender identities feel recognized, respected, and included.

What You and Your School Can Do

Of course, not all schools have the freedom or leeway to recognize or accommodate student sexual orientations or gender
identities that are anything other than normative heterosexual,
cisgender ones. Restricting those schools can be anything from
school policy to state law. For instance, as with the school I ref-
erenced earlier, a school's religious affiliation and mission may
preclude the full acknowledgment and inclusion of students
who expressed a gender identity different from their birth sex.

There are also new laws, like the one recently passed in
Florida, which curtails the discussion of sexual orientation or
gender identity in the classroom and requires parents be noti-
fied should their child receive mental health services at school.
Though the law specifies that it only applies to students in grades
K-3, many teachers at higher grade levels are concerned that it
affects their ability to discuss these issues with students as well.
And, of course, while K-3 students are not thinking about their
sexuality, some of them have parents, siblings, other relatives,
or family friends who identify as LGBTQIA2S+. This is another
way that classroom life is complicated by broader social and
political issues.

While always taking care to adhere to your school's policy
and state law, there are things you and your school community
can do to create a more inclusive and respectful environment for
students of all sexual preferences and gender identities:

Educate Yourself and, If Possible, Your Peers on LGBTQIA2S+ Issues

You've already made a great first step toward this goal by simply
reading this chapter. Now, you can keep the momentum going
by making a point to keep current on the language, the emerging
trends, and the relevant issues of sexuality, gender, and all things
LGBTQIA2S+—especially those embraced by Gen Z.

For a riveting exploration of today's gendered social norms
and dating behavior among high-school and college students,

check out Peggy Orenstein's books, *Girls & Sex* and *Boys & Sex*. Orenstein's interview subjects talk about a lot more than sex—they reveal a tremendous amount the ways in which the current generation's gender norms impact students' emotional lives and relationships, including how gender influences emotional health, coping styles, and the expression of mental health issues today.

Check Your Own Life Experiences, Identities, and Biases

For thousands of years, our society has been organized around strict definitions of gender. It's just in recent decades this has started to loosen. Thus, biases around sex and gender have become engrained in our thinking in ways we're not aware of. Even when we can intellectually understand and accept more expansive definitions of sex and gender, often our emotions are trying to catch up—which keeps us a bit off balance. All we can really do to combat our biases is to make ourselves aware of them.

However you personally identify, take some time to think about how you arrived at knowing who you are. If you are heterosexual and cisgendered, maybe you never even questioned your sexual preferences or gender. That's something worth exploring right now as well.

As you look over your own journey, notice any biases you might have about those who are different from you. Bring them into your frontal cortex, where you can think about them and own them. This way, when a student needs you, you can make sure your biases no longer interfere with your intention to support them.

Stay Attuned to Those Teaching Moments

Acts of discrimination based on sex or gender identities are moments for you to help your students think both deeper and more broadly about their own views. Everything from refusing to partner on a project with a transgender classmate to taunting an athlete on the field by saying, "you throw like a girl," are golden opportunities to make students aware of their own biases, to help them to question them, and to support students as they move toward a conclusion that better reflects their intentions for themselves and the world around them.

Check Your Course Material for Bias and Inclusion

Just as you did for racial, cultural, and socio-economic traits, review your course material for diversity and inclusion in the areas of sexuality and gender identity. No matter the subject, students in the twenty-first century deserve to be exposed to ideas and voices beyond those of straight, white men.

Recently, when I asked a group of student leaders to critique a presentation of mine, they pointed out that while my talk wasn't outright discriminatory, it was heteronormative. I was grateful for (if initially surprised by) their observations and used them to make my talk more inclusive, which made it better.

If your state laws or school policy doesn't allow for overt inclusion when it comes to LGBTQIA2S+, at the very least ensure your course material does not insult or stigmatize these populations.

Affinity Groups for LGBTQIA2S+ Students and Allies

At one high school where I consulted, a veteran teacher who identified as lesbian, started the school's gay-lesbian affinity group in the 1980s. According to her, it was a rough start. She made an announcement at a morning assembly, saying that if anyone was interested in talking about being gay or lesbian, or questioning their identity in this way, she would be right down the block at a local coffee shop at lunchtime.

She recollected that she sat at that coffee shop by herself for a week and then a month. Then one day, a student appeared. And then another. By the time she retired, in the 2010s, the school had a vibrant, student-run affinity group where students openly talked about their sexual orientations and gender identities. Eventually, students who viewed themselves as "allies" participated as well.

Today, such affinity groups can be found in many schools and many communities. Studies have shown these groups reduce stigma, as well as mental health issues and suicide rates among students who identify as LGBTQIA2S+. They also provide all students a safe environment in which to ask questions.

If it's legal at your school, an affinity group for your LGBTQIA2S+ communities and allies can be a real positive and a great resource for all students.

All You Have to Be Is There

While gender identity may represent a transitional space on the path through adolescent development, it's essential that we adults don't treat students' exploration of their gender identity as a "phase" they'll outgrow or forsake. Gen Z students experience and conceive of gender identity and sexual orientation in a more complex and nuanced way than your generation or mine. So, no matter where we personally fall along the spectrum of sex or gender identity, we must never discount where the kids we teach are in any given moment or where they might be headed.

In my own practice, I've worked with adolescents who have questioned their gender identity and subsequently pursued hormonal intervention to transition to the opposite gender. I've also seen students move from questioning and experimenting with their gender identity to settling into their birth-assigned gender in a singular and comfortable way.

When it comes to sexual orientation and gender identity, what might be most useful to us as educators is to take the stance of curiosity, to let students educate us about how they are thinking about and experiencing their evolving identities, to take their exploration at face value, and to see their struggles from their point of view. When it comes to sex and gender, we must respect our students enough to open our own minds, so we are able hear them and be there for them as they unravel these complex, fraught matters for themselves.

Talk It Out: A Scenario and Questions for Discussion

Just as in previous chapters, read through the scenario below. Then answer the questions that follow on your own or with a group of colleagues.

You are the middle school boys' soccer coach. You can easily relate to your student-athletes and enjoy friendly relationships with them. They remind you very much of yourself at their age. When you encounter them in a large group in the locker room after practice, you barely even register their constant joking and banter. It's just background noise, familiar and comfortable. One day, the school nurse approaches you after he has gone into the locker room to deliver some first-aid supplies while the sixth-grade boys are getting ready for practice. He tells you that he was concerned to hear many of the boys loudly calling each other "gay," a label clearly intended as a taunt or insult. He seems shaken to have heard this kind of language and tone from your players. You're kind of surprised, mostly because you haven't really been listening. You find it easy to believe your colleague's report. You also remember that even on your college soccer team, players threw around words like this that would now be considered homophobic.

Discussion Questions

1 Does this story sound familiar or believable to you in your current school context? Or in another school you've attended or worked in?

2 How do you understand the boys' behavior? What are the developmental and social contexts to consider?

3 What do you say to the school nurse?

4 What might you do or say re: this information? Is there anyone else with whom you want to share it?

5 Can you think of any action steps you would like to take, or have someone else in your school community take? What challenges or barriers might arise if you try to take any particular step?

Bibliography

1) Pew Research Center. (2020) On the Cusp of Adulthood and Facing an Uncertain Future: What We Know about Generation Z So Far.
2) Seemiller, Corey and Grace, Meghan. (2016) *Generation Z Goes to College.* John Wiley and Sons.
3) Trevor Project National Survey. (2021) https://www.thetrevorproject.org/survey-2021/

8

Crisis

Ever since it happened, I've never thought about my own life in the same way.

    – College sophomore, referring about his best friend's suicide when they were in high school

In the ATM booth around the corner from my house during the early hours of the day, the sun pours through the glass in a way that makes it hard to remain there for more than a few minutes without breaking into a sweat—even on a crisp New England morning. Ten years ago, on just such a morning, I was inside that booth withdrawing some cash when my cell phone rang. It was the parent of one of my students.

"I'm calling with bad news," she said, "Sarah killed herself last night."

Sarah—her son's girlfriend and also a student at our school—was in tenth grade. She was a star student, an accomplished artist, a treasured classmate. As the school counselor, I was aware she'd been struggling emotionally and seeing a private therapist, but

DOI: 10.4324/9781003358923-10

neither her friend's mother, her own parents, nor I ever anticipated this outcome. Of course, we hardly ever would.

When Crisis Comes

Throughout this book, I've emphasized that a healthy, strong
school community thrives on connection. This is a net positive.
However, it also means that when a crisis strikes one member of
that community, it's impossible for students, faculty, and staff
to escape the impact. Concentric circles of connection ripple out
across the school community and beyond.

In most cases, these aren't just fading layers of distress.
Even in circumstances less grave than a student death, these
dynamic social forces interact with one another. They are intensi-
fied because adolescents in general are exquisitely sensitive to
the reactions of their peers, as well as the adults in their midst.
Distress, fear, and confusion become contagious.

Crisis can descend on your campus from regional events
outside your school community and beyond your control—an
external crisis. For instance, Hurricane Katrina in 2005 left every
aspect of New Orleans and the Gulf States region reeling. And no
one escaped the trauma caused by the COVID-19 pandemic. As
part of those broader events, school communities were and are
affected in their own particular ways.

Crisis can also stem from the actions of someone or something
inside the school community—an internal crisis. For instance, a
mass shooting, like the ones that happened at Columbine High
School in Colorado in 1999, Sandy Hook Elementary School in
Connecticut in 2012, Stoneman Douglas High School in Parkland,
Florida in 2018, and at Robb Elementary School in Uvalde, Texas
in 2022. While the repercussions of such a tragedy may be felt
by those far outside the school, members of the school community—students, teachers, parents, staff—absorb the brunt of the
shock. I will note here that while school shootings have increased

with horrifying frequency (and one is, of course, far too many), they do remain statistically unusual.

The internal crisis most common to middle and high schools—and so the type you'll likely encounter during your career—is a student death, resulting from an accident, violence, suicide, or, in rarer cases, illness. When such a tragedy happens to a young person—a child—it affects the school community in both acute and enduring ways.

Student suicide in particular generates complex fallout for the community to process, bringing about matters of privacy, guilt, blame, and fear. Common issues when suicide occurs include faculty and staff feeling they should have been able to prevent the death, and feeling angry with the deceased for causing their own death. We also can be angry at people who die from more typical causes like old age or terminal cancer. But the psychological experience of those left behind after a teenager dies of suicide remains even more complicated than when the death is due to another cause.

No matter the crisis or its origins, don't underestimate your school's potential to mitigate the effects of the crisis for your students. As people in the world, we have little control over whether or when a crisis occurs. But we can control how we support our students and colleagues through it. As an educator, you can play a role in your school's response.

A Range of Reactions

In season one of the Netflix series *13 Reasons Why* (the fictional) Liberty High School's response to the suicide of student Hannah Baker is a useful lesson in how a school should *not* respond to a crisis. Most objectionable, the show glamorizes teen suicide, e.g., with students decorating Hannah's locker as a memorial and, of course, by featuring the mysterious cassette tapes where Hannah has explained her "reasons" for dying.

The series also misrepresents many aspects of suicide, including (ironically) the "reasons" for it and the role depression may or may not play. While there are a variety of explanations as to why Hannah's classmates do not fare well in the wake of the crisis, the most glaring is that the adult characters—including the school counselor—fail to address their needs.

Developing supportive responses to students after a crisis begins with understanding how adolescents react to and process grief, trauma, or other major events that, while not as serious, affect school life. Adolescents do not have the perspective adults have. The more fortunate ones haven't yet had to navigate serious losses.

Grief is rarely a linear process, and each of us goes through it in our own way. This is especially true for adolescents, who—as we've discussed—vary widely in their level of cognitive, emotional, and social development. Like all of us, students are likely to experience psychologist Elizabeth Kubler-Ross' iconic five stages of grief: denial, anger, bargaining, depression, and acceptance. Just not in any specific order and not in a predetermined amount of time.

Any of these five grief stages can resurface at any time for years to come. As a student's mind matures and new functions come online, they often re-process major life events. So a crisis that happened in tenth grade can trigger thoughts or manifest in behaviors in twelfth grade. It's useful to keep this in mind when trying to understand the underlying issues behind a student's presentation or behavior, even quite a while after a major crisis.

We also need to remember that students—like all of us—bring their whole selves to how they view and come to terms with a crisis. After the suicide at my school, the impact on Sarah's close friends was profound. That I expected. I was also advised to be concerned for and to keep a close watch on any students who were already struggling with self-injury and suicidal thoughts, even those outside Sarah's circle of friends.

To my initial surprise, however, several students with no prior mental health issues and no relationship with Sarah showed signs of severe distress as well. I was especially confounded by one student who was deeply affected by the suicide though I knew he didn't know Sarah at all. Then, I realized his father had died suddenly the previous year. It was no wonder this second unexpected death in his young life brought up feelings of grief and visceral fear for him.

I also witnessed some students return to their daily routines almost immediately after their classmate's suicide. I even noticed some joking around and laughing. At first, I was troubled, as my own mood was deeply and pervasively somber. Then I had to remind myself to stop looking through my adult-centric lens. Everything a teenager feels is right there on the surface, even though they might be expressing it in a way that looks "inappropriate" to us. Whether it was a psychological defense, a search for the comfort of familiarity, or simply an adolescent ability to tune out a major crisis, I came to see my students' "getting back to it" or "picking up where they'd left off" as one more "normal" response to a terribly abnormal situation.

The lesson here was that I had to make room in my own processing to allow for each student to cope in their own way. This was also true for my colleagues. We all had different mechanisms, paces, and styles as we reacted to our collective loss.

How to Prepare Your School for Crisis

As I stood, half-baked by the sun and wholly stunned by the phone call in the ATM booth that morning, questions cascaded into my head. Many, I knew, would need to be answered sooner, rather than later.

- ◆ Do we cancel classes tomorrow?
- ◆ How—and what—do we communicate to students and families?

◆ What about Sarah's closest friends? Do we reach out to them individually?

It happened to be the Monday of a holiday weekend. Mercifully, this afforded about twelve hours total to gather my thoughts, see if I could solicit some expert advice, and confer with my school leadership and faculty about how to handle this. We'd never experienced anything like this before. And, of course, it was the very worst thing.

As I struggled with my own emotional reaction, a counselor from another local school who had heard about Sarah's death reached out to offer her condolences and support. While her school had not experienced a suicide, they'd had other crises recently and she knew it would help me to have someone who understood. It really did.

I was also able to contact a nationally prominent suicide expert who had recently retired from practice—perhaps that's why he actually picked up the phone when I called. As soon as I explained what had happened, he sprang into action, telling me what we should do—and not do—in the next twenty-four hours.

My learning curve was steep. But with the expert's guidance, my own inside knowledge of our school community, and our "multidisciplinary squad" of educators and administrators, we came up with a plan for shepherding our school through this crisis. Here's what we did:

Consult with the Survivors

No matter the crisis, the first step in any crisis plan is contacting the victims to ensure any actions you take are supportive of them and certainly do not add to their pain.

When the crisis is a student suicide, the school counselor or designated administrator (often the head or principal) will contact the family, offer their condolences, and ask for their input on the school's approach. In a highly sensitive situation, if your school has a communications professional, they will also likely be involved. Of course, as a teacher, you will not be the one expected to handle "Big Picture" conversations or decisions.

A complication that often arises in a case of student suicide is that the family wants privacy concerning their child's death. In this case, the school must respect the family's wishes, while still doing whatever possible to console and protect all its students.

Sarah's parents were very direct in sharing information with us. Their daughter had left a suicide note. They permitted us to share the cause of Sarah's death with students and other parents in the interest of transparency and as an alert to adolescent suicide risk.

The family also wanted us to let Sarah's friends and teachers know they were welcome to visit them at home. For Sarah's family, being in the presence of those who also knew and loved their daughter was welcome. Not all families feel this way. When in doubt, as an institution or an individual, just ask what would be helpful and what might not be welcome.

Communicate

The most common complaints schools get from students and parents after a crisis are lack of communication and lack of transparency. Of course, sometimes the school doesn't have the information they're seeking. Or you, as a teacher, don't have it, even if your administration does. For example, in the case of a student death, it might not be clear whether a student died by suicide or by accident, such as when there's a car accident or a drug overdose.

A death is a profound loss. To a certain extent, the cause doesn't matter and certainly doesn't change things. However, when there is ambiguity, human nature dictates that there will be speculation, anxiety, and rumors complicating the social and emotional landscape, none of which is healthy or productive for a school community. It's important to quell that as much and as quickly as possible. The clearer the school can be in communicating what has happened, the better.

After Sarah's death, we consulted with her family and decided to send out a memo immediately to the entire school community—students, parents, and staff—informing them of her passing. The first school day after the suicide, we held an assembly, where we again went over what had happened. We also let our students know they were invited by the family— but not required by us—to attend Sarah's funeral service. We informed them that the school would be providing transportation, so we could attend as a collective.

Increase Counseling and Monitoring

Making counseling available and easy to access not only eases student distress, it can prevent more serious problems and another crisis from happening.

To that end, we increased the number of hours our school counseling office was open and made clear to our students and staff that no appointment was necessary—they could just drop in. To further strengthen this mental health effort, teachers circumscribed periods during classes to check in. They also decreased the pressure on students by allowing for more flexibility in homework, tests, and deadlines.

In addition, our counseling team tracked Sarah's close friends and all students with a known history of depression, self-harm, or suicidal thinking. This meant being more transparent with our faculty about individual students' emotional vulnerabilities, as well as staying in closer touch with their parents via phone consultations.

To parents who were concerned about their child's privacy, I personally explained that, because our teachers were so shaken and frightened by Sarah's death, I needed, much more than usual, to be able to assure them that certain students were "safe." I needed to be able to explain unusual behaviors or presentations as fully as possible.

Our student support and administrative teams also took special care, once we had space and time, to review our protocols and resources for intervening with students with mental health needs.

Hold a Parent Meeting (or Two)

Whatever the crisis, parents are going to have questions they may not want to discuss in front of their children. So holding a parent meeting on the topic with a specialist who can address their concerns makes good sense.

About a week after Sarah's funeral, we invited parents to a private forum with a youth suicide and grief specialist. Along with faculty and administrators, I participated in the meeting and made myself available to answer questions both that night and later in the week.

The meeting also provided a safe space for all of us adults to talk about our (adult) fears, as well as our grief and concern for Sarah's family.

Do Not Hold a Public Memorial at School for at Least One Year

This step is specific to student suicide. Unlike other deaths, suicide carries the grave risk of contagion or "copycat" acts by other students. Vulnerable students may be drawn to the positive attention that the deceased child receives. Memorials may inadvertently "glamorize" suicide, even though their purpose is to remember and honor the child who has died.

Students were surprised, confused, and resentful when we told them they could not immediately create a memorial at the school. What we did do is create a permanent display of their classmate's art.

Then, a year later, we held a remembrance of Sarah's life. We did not cancel classes or change the structure of the day. We identified a room where students could drop in throughout the course of the school day and right after school to play music, write, create art, and talk. As I had expected, there was no predictable pattern to which students showed up there. A number of students found it helpful to have a place to remember their friend and classmate.

Your Crisis Is Unique to You

My experience with a suicide at our school allowed me to advise other schools where such an unimaginable crisis has occurred. And though I could advise, I always cautioned—as I was cautioned—that your school crisis is unique to your school. Every community is different. What matters most—no matter how grave the situation—is the sincerity and appropriateness of the school's response.

School, like no other place in a child's life, has the ability to right their course when they are experiencing a crisis. Author and educator Karen Gross, who we talked about in Chapter 4, speaks of the five elements necessary for a trauma-responsive school. She calls them the Five Ss: Stability, Structure, Safety, Subtlety, and Someone(s) (Gross, 2020).

Whatever else is going on in their lives, most students can depend on school for stability, structure, and safety. For many students, school provides a place of certainty in a turbulent world. For teens especially, school is also where they find that "someone," a counselor or teacher they can turn to in times of crisis. The "subtlety" Gross speaks of is the skill we worked on in the earlier chapters in this section. It's our ability to see our students as the individuals they are, to meet them where they are, and to help them through the crisis in the way that's right for them.

How to Prepare Yourself

If a crisis strikes your school, there's a chance you'll be asked to weigh in on the school's response plan or perhaps serve on the crisis team. But no matter what your role is on a macro or institutional level, your most important contributions will be found in smaller, private moments with individual students. As no one else in their life, you have the potential to mitigate the effects of crisis for your students by simply being present when they need you.

Because of their developmental phase, middle-school—and to a greater extent, high-school—students may not want to share their reactions to a crisis with their parents. Especially in the case of a loss or trauma that affects your school community, students may seek out you, their teacher, because you are to some extent "in it together." You may also find yourself more drawn to support, care for, or "check on" your students during a time of crisis.

Virtually none of us is trained in how to respond to crisis, at least not routinely. But sticking to some basic tenets can provide purpose and direction as you are called upon to help students and families in your midst. The job here mostly comes down to listening.

After a crisis, expect students to approach you after class or in the hallway to talk about what happened. If you want to be a resource for them, you must be prepared to hear and receive their anxieties and fears, both rational and not. You must be open to hearing things that might make you uncomfortable or even worried. If you do hear something from a student that alerts you to a potential problem or risk, do not worry alone. Find another teacher or the school counselor and share your concern. Better yet, if your school has a protocol for such issues, follow that.

In these encounters, be willing to share your own perspectives and reactions—but in judicious doses. Before you share, ask yourself, "Am I sharing my own experience because it will help my student or because I need someone to talk to?"

For example, if the crisis is a suicide, it's fine to say how sad you are about the student who died. You can even relate that you went through a peer suicide when you were in high school. But don't talk about your own struggles in this area or delve into too many details about your own feelings. Use your own friends and family, as well as your colleagues, for comfort. You never want a student to feel like they need to take care of you.

After the student suicide at my school, it was actually another student with whom I felt the strongest connection in terms of our respective emotional reactions to the situation. But I didn't tell him so. That kind of self-disclosure would have been too personal, a crossing of a boundary. I simply noted it to myself, with both surprise and appreciation.

During a crisis even more than any other time, remember that parents need to be kept in the loop. In the case of a student suicide, parents will be, understandably, on high alert, even if their own children haven't previously shown signs of distress or depression. As we discussed in the opening chapter, students view you as an "expert" across many domains. To some extent, parents do too. And that's even truer in a time of crisis when emotions are heightened and everyone is looking for comfort and guidance. As parents try to understand their own reactions, they need advice about how to comfort their own children. As an educator, expect to be asked to step into this role, even though you may also be grieving, frightened, and confused.

Secondary Trauma and Compassion Fatigue

What's important is that you find ways to be there for both students and parents without becoming burdened with the emotional responsibility. If you don't want to be a resource for your students in times of crisis, it's perfectly acceptable and advisable for you to refer students to a school counselor or administrator. You should also feel free to look to these same colleagues for support for yourself if you need it. In the aftermath of the student suicide, I spent a good deal of my time supporting our teachers in their grief, so they would be able to support their students in more meaningful ways.

Secondary trauma and compassion fatigue are real for teachers. No one need look any further than our schools during the COVID-19 crisis to see that. Because self-care is paramount and yet elusive for educators, schools should be proactive in this area. In addition to equipping faculty and staff with knowledge and skills through professional development and collective conversation, schools would do well to provide stress management resources, offer as much flexibility as feasible (re: schedules and job details), and promote practices and policies that support the adults on campus so they don't burn out.

A Turning Point

As I considered how I might shape this chapter, I found myself looking up "crisis" in the Oxford English Dictionary. The meaning was pretty much what you'd expect: "a. a time of intense difficulty, trouble, or danger," and "b. a time when a difficult or important decision must be made." But the synonym struck me as worth sharing: "Synonym: a turning point."

This synonym suggests that a crisis is a moment where it matters what we do. Our response can take the situation in one direction or another, for better or worse. And when that direction involves our students' lives and their ability to not only come through but become resilient in the face of crisis—well, the stakes of getting this right couldn't be higher.

Talk It Out: A Scenario and Questions for Discussion

Read through the scenario below. Then answer the questions that follow yourself or with a group of colleagues.

You teach high school. A colleague and friend who teaches at another high school across town informs you that one of their students, Maggie, has just died by suicide. Your colleague tells you to keep this information to yourself, especially as it's not yet clear whether the cause of Maggie's death is being identified publicly. Also, Maggie has a younger sibling in their school community.

It turns out that Maggie was a well-known soccer player with numerous athletic and social connections with students at your school. As you're preparing for an advisory session with a handful of your students already in the room, you hear one of them announcing Maggie's death to the other students. They are debating why such an awesome athlete and great kid would want to die. They speculate that it had to do with her losing out on a recruitment offer from her first-choice college. One of the students also mentions that the deceased student was "hooking up" with a boy at your school, a student you have taught in the past and know well.

What do you do?

Discussion Questions

1 What do you do/say in response to what you overhear in the moment in advisory?
2 What steps, if any, might you take after your advisory session is over?
3 What else would you want to know if you found yourself in this situation? How might you obtain this information? Are there any barriers to gathering it?
4 Would you consider reaching out to a counselor, administrator or another colleague to discuss what you heard in your advisory? If so, who?
5 Is there any reason to reach out to the boy who is described as "hooking up" with Maggie, or to his family? Or to identify him to a counselor, administrator, or another colleague?
6 Are there any implications for your own school community in terms of what should be announced, discussed, or addressed? What do you think should happen next?

Bibliography

1) Gross, Karen. (2020) *Trauma Doesn't Stop at the School Door: Strategies and Solutions for Educators, Pre-K – College.* Teachers College Press. Columbia University.

Section III
Strengthening Their Circle of Support

9

Meet the Parents

A child psychiatrist gets off a phone call, visibly exasperated by the conversation she's just finished, and exclaims, "Why can't I get any patients with normal parents?"

– An old joke

As an educator, how would you describe the ideal parent for your students? One who is loving, supportive, and patient? Who highly values education but defers to your judgment about curriculum, assessment methods, and grading? Respects you and your colleagues? Is engaged, yet stays out of the way?

The good news is that a large proportion of parents in your school community will come close to fitting this description. The bad news? Some won't. Through my experience, I've settled on a rule of thumb that I share with teachers called the 80/20 rule: 20 percent of parents will take up 80 percent of your time and energy; and 80 percent of parents will take up 20 percent.

Regardless of the portion of the distribution into which a given parent falls, it's essential to cultivate a relationship

DOI: 10.4324/9781003358923-12

with all parents. This isn't necessarily intuitive nor is it always easy. You're probably not trained for it, nor did you explicitly agree to take them on. But parents, it turns out, are vital to an educator's job.

Part of the reason for this is that parents are arguably the most important people in your students' lives. Even as your students roll their eyes, sigh in exasperation, and assert that their parents know nothing, most adolescents are actively seeking their parents' affection and acceptance. Sometimes, the students with the most limited or troubled parents yearn for these things the most deeply. As a therapist, I am reminded of this on a regular basis. In one recent exchange I had with a tenth grader she exclaimed, "I'm kind of done with my dad. He is so problematic." And then, not five minutes later, she mused, "I think what I really want most is my dad's approval."

Regardless of the quality of a family's relationships, it behooves teachers, as it does child psychologists, to forge connections and invest in relationships with parents. They can be your natural allies. After all, they are on the front line too, with children they may not understand. When carefully tended, the parent-teacher relationship can provide all adult parties with crucial information and collaboration when they're most necessary. A lack of relationship, on the other hand, can result in ineffective communication—or even confrontation or rupture—that interferes with your student's best interest.

In my line of work, I've caused myself plenty of totally avoidable problems by not tending to the parent relationship. I once worked with an eighth grader, Ben, who was an anxious, tentative kid, and a brilliant humanities student. When it came time for him to register for courses for the upcoming semester, he told me his mother was insisting he take advantage of an elective computer coding course his school offered. Ben then confided in me that he really didn't want to take this course. At all. He simply wasn't interested in coding. Further, he didn't want the elective to detract from his time for other coursework. However, consistent with a pattern of which we were both aware, Ben was intimidated by his mother's forceful style. Ben told me he wanted to stand up to his mother but wasn't sure he could.

After reviewing his other classes and activities with him, I could see that Ben was indeed already overcommitted in terms of academics, athletics, and his school commute. In my professional opinion, he needed to prioritize work-life balance—and assert himself to his mother. To me, these practical and developmental priorities were more important for him at this moment than learning to code. I encouraged Ben to stand up to his mother regarding his wish to decline this course.

He did. And she promptly stopped speaking to me.

Well, not right away. First, she called me. When I registered her tone of voice, I asked whether she was angry with me. She responded with a stony silence that felt like it lasted five minutes, but probably didn't. She then launched into a lecture about the fact that STEM classes (science, technology, engineering, and math) were a high priority in their household. Ben's mother sincerely believed that if her son didn't take this ninth-grade coding elective, he would not be able to compete in the "STEM-centric world of the future."

That was the last conversation she and I had for about six months.

I didn't agree with Ben's mother's reasoning or approach then, nor do I now. But I'd clearly made a mistake. I was so aligned and identified with Ben that I neglected to consider my relationship with his mother. I should have spoken to her first, offline, about my concerns, rather than stepping into the middle of their family.

The important side note to my snafu with Ben's mother was that it also provided me with insight, via direct experience, into why Ben was so reluctant—frightened, really—to go against his mother's wishes. If I had made the effort to know her; my knowledge would have then informed my work with Ben.

To her credit, Ben's mother continued to drive him to his meetings with me and pay my bill promptly. This gave me yet another perspective on her. She recognized that Ben's work with me was extremely important to him. She loved him enough to continue to support our relationship, despite her personal misgivings about my approach.

Taking Charge of the Relationship

While cultivating a positive working relationship with parents makes perfect sense and certainly sounds great, if you've been teaching for a while, you might be thinking, "Parents are intimidating, and they can be so unreasonable or, "I signed up to work with kids, not parents. "Or even," If I had my choice, I'd rather not deal with parents at all."

Unfortunately, as you've already figured out, educators don't really have a choice here. You have to engage with your students' parents. So, you might as well make the interface as productive and beneficial as possible.

Most of the tension I witness between parents and teachers results from real or perceived differences in priorities—just as with Ben's mother and me. While both parents and teachers want what's best for the student, they don't always agree on what "best" looks like, or the means by which it should be achieved. Teachers and other professionals may disagree with parents about which skills and competencies are most important, what behaviors and personality traits should be encouraged, and what teaching methods are optimal for reaching a student/child.

In addition, parents naturally have a host of expectations, anxieties, and fears when it comes to their child's education. They are sending their child off into this other world for the whole day, and in many cases not getting much intel back. Because they are so deeply emotionally invested, the stakes are high for them. All of these factors contribute to a dramatic backdrop before parents even meet you.

In order to build a foundation of mutual trust and collaboration, make the first move and invite parents onto your team. Reassure them that you recognize and know their child. Clarify for them what happens in your classroom. Tell them you are interested in their concerns. Let them know your door is always open. Make them feel comfortable with you and confident in your expertise before they have any reason to doubt you.

Now, you may encounter a tiny minority of parents who are not able to trust you or your school. In these rare cases, their lack of trust may be a longstanding characteristic that far predates their relationship with you. I remember one mother from my time as a school counselor who was never satisfied with anything her son Nate's teachers (or our administration, or I) did on his behalf. Despite spending lots of time on him (and her), none of us could seem to satisfy what she felt were her son's needs.

Shortly before pulling her son out of our school, she barked at me heatedly, "I'll have you know, this was not our first-choice school for Nate." Remaining ever open and curious, I promptly inquired, "Oh, what was your first-choice school?" She hesitated for a moment, seeming momentarily flustered, before blurting out, "Well, we didn't have one!"

In a situation like this, you really can't take rejection personally. And unless you've done something truly thoughtless or problematic, you rarely should. Some parents are simply fighting battles you can't even know about.

Taking charge of your relationships with parents takes time and effort, but it actually saves both in the long run. If you're not sure of how to build relationships with parents, use the advice in this chapter, and also ask a more experienced colleague or a wise administrator at your school how they do it, what they've learned about what works—and, of course, what doesn't.

Partnership and Collaboration

When I tell people I specialize in counseling teenagers, I invariably encounter a mixture of surprise, horror, gratitude ("Better you than me"), and—occasionally— admiration. Some adults are impressed for the simple reason that many of them consider teenagers at best a mystery and at worst a cultural affliction. While parents may find their own teenagers more compelling than adolescents at large, others find their own even harder to take.

Because, like me, you work with adolescents every day, you know things about them that other adults—including their parents—cannot. You know how they learn. You know how thoughtful, funny, and sweet they can be. You know how clear-eyed they are, unencumbered by the defenses many of us adults have developed due to weariness and the passage of time. On a good day, you genuinely enjoy your students. Even if you don't always understand them, you are interested in their minds and a keen observer of their lives. Over the course of your career, you're likely to help usher hundreds of adolescents toward adulthood. This distinguishes you from most adults. It also puts you in a unique position to help them—the other adults, that is.

Even highly competent and involved parents are often bewildered or overwhelmed by teenagers. Though I am an adolescent psychologist, I have repeatedly found myself "surprised" when my own daughter demonstrates perfectly predictable moves in a new phase of development. Do I know that neglecting to consult me before making decisions or finding me "annoying" are normal for a teenager and supposed to happen? Well, yes, I've learned—and taught many others—these very notions. Do I still get hurt, disappointed, even dismayed when she displays these developmentally on-target behaviors? Indeed. I'm a person, after all.

Parents' personalities, daily lives, histories, and relationships with their children are complex and, at times, confusing, stressful, and even painful. And most parents don't have any education or training in adolescent psychology. Knowing they're partnering with someone with your experience, someone who has made a career out of getting through to adolescents, can be a great comfort for them. Knowing they have you in their corner, as well as their child's, can reduce their anxiety. Even if you're a young or beginning teacher, parents will look to you as an expert. Keep in mind that you know more than you think you do, and you likely know more—at least about adolescents—than many parents do.

On the other side of this collaboration, you can benefit from the depth of knowledge about your students that only a parent can have. Parents have, of course, been there from the beginning. They know their child's developmental history, their personality traits, and—if they're reasonably tuned in— their strengths and vulnerabilities. They may know what tends to set their child off and what helps settle them down. They know what their child is like at home. (Even if the kid is always behind a closed door in their room wearing headphones, that's still information.)

Developing a friendly, productive give-and-take with parents requires showing them that you are allies in a joint endeavor: the education and development of their child. Earning parents' trust comes down to managing the relationship with care and skill from the start.

Your Parent Management Kit

To that end, here are some basic guidelines for establishing collaborative relationships with your students' parents:

Restore Parents' Confidence

Many parents felt competent—even expert—at raising their children in the elementary school years. But around seventh or eighth grade (sometimes earlier), many parents find that what

used to work is suddenly inadequate, their expertise now virtually defunct. At this point, many parents fear that they're not up
to the task of raising a teenager.

Some parents worry that you, a professional educator, are
judging them, even if it's not the case. They may be embarrassed
or feel it's their fault if their child is acting out, struggling academically, not fitting in. And some parents carry negative school
experiences from their own childhoods or complicated feelings
about authority figures. Regardless of whether you feel like one,
you are an authority figure to not only students, but to parents.
In a parent's view, you hold the fate of their child in your hands.
They're in a vulnerable spot.

If parents express feelings of inadequacy when it comes to
their teenager, let them know their feelings are normal. They
only know their own adolescent child—you know many. They
may not have time to talk with other parents about what it's like
to have a teenager—you talk to many parents about it. You can
contextualize certain typical behaviors or attitudes for them in
a way few other adults can. Explain to them that because their
child is developing, their parental role is in flux as well—and
that's why they feel unsteady. Remind them that you are here,
not only as a resource for their child, but for them should they
have questions or concerns.

Reassure Parents about Their Child Whenever Possible

If you have ushered your own child through adolescence, you
know that all parents really want is to know that their child is
okay—or at the very least, will be okay eventually. Some parents
want reassurance that their child is the "best," but most parents
of teenagers set the bar at a more reasonable point. So, if you can
honestly say that a student is on track and, while there may be
some issues, they are likely to be just fine, make sure you say
so. If indicated (and true), let parents know their child is within
the realm of "typical" for their age—though make sure parents

understanding that "typical" can span a broad range. If there is a problem, let them know you are prepared to help them address it or identify colleagues who can.

Take Cultural and Social-class Preferences into Account

As discussed in the previous section of this book, whenever you are addressing parents, be sure to consider how their identities may affect their point of view. Think about the racial, cultural, or social-class factors that may go into their decision-making, parenting styles, and expectations for their child. Check your own identity and blind spots in these same areas. From an open and thoughtful place regarding differences, you are more likely to figure out how best to communicate productively with parents. If you're curious or confused about something, ask about it.

When I was a school counselor, I encountered a pair of parents who could not consider that their child needed to see a therapist for his anxiety and depression. Needing therapy was seen as a sign of weakness in their culture. After listening to them, I could hear that they not only feared that counseling would label their child, but also that it would be a distraction and prevent their child from achieving academically—the latter being the all-important priority for them.

So, I reframed the conversation. I let the parents know that anxiety and depression, if untreated, can impede academic performance. I explained that poor concentration, low energy, and disrupted sleep—all physical symptoms that result from anxiety and depression—could interfere with their son's studying and test taking. Therapy would not only improve his mood and reduce his anxiety, it would likely increase his concentration, organization, and stamina, thereby improving his performance. Finally, I encouraged them to talk with their son's trusted pediatrician to verify my advice.

When in doubt, just *listen* to parents. Even if you've heard troubling things about them—and even if they really are prickly or demanding—listening enables you to learn about your student's family context. And it may help you consider a more fitting remedy or next step than you could have done without this information. In addition to expanding your understanding, listening also makes parents feel heard, and can enhance their trust in and ability to partner with you.

Avoid These Common Pitfalls

In all relationships there are pitfalls to be avoided. In the parent-teacher relationship, these snares are mostly the result of us educators unknowingly tapping into a parent's vulnerability and putting them on the defensive. To avoid doing so, try following these guidelines.

♦ Don't underestimate the power of conversation. Pick up the phone or invite parents in. Working together and comparing notes freely (in real time), parents and teachers can do more for a student than either can alone.

♦ Don't criticize a student unnecessarily. Say something positive for every concerning or upsetting observation you share. Whenever you enter an interaction with a parent, speak of their child as if that child were your own—with understanding, assuming the best, and wanting the best for them.

♦ Don't be afraid to share what you observe. However, stick to what you know. Describe behaviors factually, providing specific examples. Offer direct quotes from the student if you have them at your disposal. You want the parent to recognize (and believe) what you are describing—and help you figure out what to do next.

♦ Don't let parents think their student is the only one with whatever issue they're facing. Provide developmental or academic context, based on the student's peer group— e.g., "We've seen this issue in a lot of ninth graders this year." This diffuses the tension immediately and allows everyone to focus on the solution.

◆ Don't make parents feel guilty. Even if you think you know better or would never do things their way, consider how you would react if someone approached you with an air of superiority. As a prospective parent, you never know what kid you're going to get. Some kids can make the most average parent look great. Others can make even a wonderful person look incompetent.

◆ Don't put yourself in the middle of family conflict. In two-parent families, parents don't always agree on key issues, especially when it comes to teenagers. "Key issues" may include (but are not limited to) academic expectations, college/career goals, substance experimentation, social life, athletic commitments, mental health, or medical care decisions. Don't take sides.

◆ Don't show your internal, emotional reactions, even if you feel attacked by a parent. The head of the high school where I worked had a rule about what to do when any of us received an angry, accusatory, or presumptuous note from a student's parent. He wisely counseled, "Respond to the email the parent should have written." I continue to find this mantra useful because it acknowledges that there are generally reasonable, substantive issues in play, however a parent packages them. A parent who is anxious, angry (not necessarily at you), upset, or in some cases merely a difficult person, may mask a legitimate concern or query in a long and unpleasant message. If this happens to you, take a moment and do the following:

1. Take a deep breath.
2. Try to consider what is behind the message (just as you might with a student).
3. Respond accordingly.

You may be able to turn down the temperature and steer the conversation back in the right direction. After all, this isn't about being right—it's about what is best for your student.

◆ Don't rely solely on your own information. Ask the parents about their experience of their child. For example, "Is what I'm describing something you've seen with Mateo in the past, when he was younger, or does it sound new? Instead of, "Has he always been this way?" Ask, "What are you seeing at home?"

The hardest conversations to have with a parent include those where their child is making inadequate academic progress, displaying aggressive behavior, seeming depressed, or even revealing self-injurious behavior. When you must have one of these conversations, start by making sure the parents understand that you're not assuming they are the problem. Convey that you regard them as a key part of the solution—and that you will work together to help their child—your student—be the best version of themselves.

Are We Talking about the Same Kid?

In my early days as a school counselor, before the advent of cloud-based records, I maintained folders for each student with whom I was working. These folders contained what you would expect: my written notes, neuropsychological testing, grades reports, and other relevant documents. I kept them in a locked steel cabinet in my office.

At the end of one day, I found myself on an extended phone call with my patient Will's mother. Will, a ninth grader, was having a host of problems with his teachers. While a bright student, he seemed to have trouble acknowledging when he got something wrong or didn't know an answer. He was also prone to quibbling with teachers over grades. For example, he'd argue they should have awarded more points on his quiz responses. With classmates, he could be a bit snappish, which appeared—at least to me—to result from a mix of insecurity and still-developing social skills.

As I tried to lay out my concerns to his mother, hoping to gain greater understanding of my student's context (and move toward recommendations), I noticed I was becoming increasingly confused by her responses. Suddenly, I had a jolting thought—was I talking to the right parent? Did I have her son mixed up with someone else? My stomach dropped.

I slowly tiptoed over to my filing cabinet, holding the phone receiver steady. (This was also pre-AirPods.) I scanned the labels for Will's last name and pulled out his folder. I felt momentarily relieved, then alarmed, and ultimately amused. I had not made a mistake. I had the right kid. His mom and I just had really different ideas about who he was.

Once I'd finished our phone call, I figured out that Will's mom's responses and perceptions were not merely a distraction—they could provide me with some clues about Will's difficulties. Will's mother had adapted to his style by accommodating his needs and kind of "glossing over" the places where his behavior was immature or even inappropriate. In fact, she herself had a milder, "adult" version of some Will's very issues.

Subsequently, I shared my observations from my phone call with Will's teachers, who seemed instantly more empathic and patient with his quirks. Ultimately, we tailored our approach with Will at school to provide structured guidance to him about understanding his grades, handling disagreements, and coping with being "wrong" sometimes. In individual counseling sessions, Will and I played out different real and hypothetical situations, including "worst-case scenarios" where conflicts arose between his ideal and the reality. His teachers found that using humor, as well as setting limits with his anxious grade-quibbling, was useful. ("Okay, you can ask me about this grade one time, and then I want to hear about the robot you're building.")

The lesson here is that, even if you are reaching out, communicating, and doing all you can to bring parents onto your team, don't assume their perceptions will coincide with your own. Even barring racial-ethnic, cultural, or simply role differences, there are times when you'll be surprised that the child the parent has in mind does not really sound like the student you're seeing every day.

It's helpful to remember that a student's behavior and presentation vary across contexts. Parents and teachers can have markedly different perceptions of and experiences with the very same kid. Asking questions, while staying open and curious, helps you learn about your student and their parents in ways that may end up explaining a lot.

Stuck in the Middle

Sometimes, however, parents don't just have a different perception, they simply do not want to engage at all, or are too self-absorbed with their own problems to put their teenager first.

I'll never forget when I found myself with Olivia, a tenth grader, in my office, while I spoke simultaneously with her father on my office phone and her mother on a cell phone. The parents were bitterly divorced. They could not agree on anything, including any academic, emotional, or practical issue pertaining to Olivia.

I can't tell you exactly how I ended up in this situation, except to say that I think Olivia was on her cell phone with her mother when her father called my line. The physical challenge of maintaining both calls, listening to each parent, and trying to respond made me feel—well—crazy. After extricating myself from this tele-triangle, I looked at Olivia, who was sitting there in her usual anxious state, though rather unsurprised by my predicament. There was not much I could say, besides, "Okay, well, I think I see what you're up against."

Our culture likes to think that parents are there for their children completely. But this isn't always true. The vast majority of parents—as I said earlier, maybe 80 percent of them—are kind, thoughtful, respectful, collaborative, and even fun. You might like to invite them out for drinks or dinner (though you should probably refrain to maintain professional boundaries). These parents put their children's needs first. They respect your authority and expertise. They are appreciative of what you and your school provide their children.

But a good 20 percent of parents are more complicated. For a wide range of very good reasons—their own anxiety, trauma history, lack of material resources, or in some cases, too many material resources and excessive privilege—they are unable to rise to the occasion where their child is concerned. They simply can't handle what parenting requires of them at this moment.

Not surprisingly, some of the children of these parents will have more issues in your classroom. While it can be frustrating, it behooves you to find a way to connect with these parents for the sake of your student. When a parent isn't the best, more of the responsibility to lead and sustain the relationship will fall on your shoulders.

Recruit Parents to Your Team

But remember, most parents will be a pleasure to know. Making an effort with them will be productive and rewarding. Open lines of communication between parents and teachers keep both on the same page, create the most supportive environment in which your students can learn and develop, and make for a better school experience for all involved. When it comes to the more difficult parents, remember that they are relying on you, too. Because you know about adolescent development, learning, and mental health, you may be able to help in ways nobody else can.

Talk It Out: A Scenario and Questions for Discussion

Read through the scenario below. Then answer the questions that follow by yourself or with a group of colleagues.

Zack, a sixth grader who seems young for his age, has always had a bit of trouble staying focused, completing assignments efficiently, and sitting still. This year, his difficulties seem more pronounced. The other day, he became so "bouncy" during your math lesson that he literally fell right out of his chair.

Zack's parents have been aware of these issues since he was in third grade through parent-teacher conferences. This year, you've already had them in twice to discuss Zack's "unusually high activity level" and the way it is affecting his classroom learning. (You wisely don't mention to them that their son's "bounciness" is also distracting to your other students.)

The school counselor has recommended—more than once—that Zack have an outside psychological evaluation to try to tease out what's driving his behavior and to generate ideas for classroom accommodations or other interventions that might help him. Zack's parents have declined to follow the school's recommendation as they don't feel there's really anything "wrong" with Zack and expect that the school should be able to handle him better.

Later in the week, in a student support team meeting, the vice principal reports that Zack's parents have come to see her. In their meeting, they told her they've been doing some reading about "boys in school" and have concluded that your school is not well versed in or tolerant enough of "typical boy behavior." They argued that your school, like many others, caters to girls, who mature earlier and are naturally more inclined to sit still and pay attention for longer periods of time. They made it clear that they are not going to have their son "labeled" by an evaluation, and if you and Zack's other teachers can't figure out how to keep their son engaged, they are going to homeschool him (which you know would make a kid as social as Zack miserable).

Discussion Questions

1 What else would you want to know if you found yourself in this situation? How might you obtain that information? Are there any barriers to gathering the information you need?

2 Would you consider pulling a colleague into the loop? If so, why and who?

3 Is there any need to involve any other administrator or colleague beyond the vice principal at this point? On what criteria do you base this decision

4 How would you respond to Zack's parents' assertions? Is there any validity to them? Do they have a point?

5 What would be your plan from here? Are there any action steps you're considering?

6 Are there any barriers to taking these steps? If so, what will factor into your decisions

7 What outcome would you hope to achieve

8 Is there anything you learned from discussing this situation that you might suggest becomes a standard school practice, or a policy?

10

Encouraging an Emotionally Healthy School

> We are expected to help our students process their reactions, but nobody has given us a forum where we can process our own.
>
> – High school faculty member re: January 6, 2021
> United States Capitol Insurrection

Creating a school environment that supports student mental health and wellbeing largely to your school leadership team. The administration should provide clear guidelines (via an official handbook, as well as real-time conversation) about exactly what to do when you're concerned about a student. It is also their responsibility to ensure that proper resources—like well-trained school counselors and a multidisciplinary student support team—are in place to work directly with students and families as well as to guide teachers and other staff members.

Still, just because something falls under a school administration's purview doesn't ensure it will be comprehensive or even

DOI: 10.4324/9781003358923-13

adequate for the evolving complexities of students' and families' needs and circumstances. While most schools recognize the necessity of tending to student wellbeing and carefully monitoring mental health concerns, not every school has yet been able to craft comprehensive policies, and many simply don't have the funding for optimal resources and staffing.

Wherever your school administration is in the course of this work, you and your colleagues can get active in encouraging your school to do more and do it better.

Needless to say, teachers don't need yet another responsibility. But doing what you can to ensure that student mental health is a priority on your campus is effort well invested, because it will bring significant return for everyone. The more thoughtful and specific the guidance in this area, and the more accessible the resources, the easier it will be for you to direct and refer students in need. With the proper support, adolescents can be remarkably resilient, even under the most strenuous circumstances, and persist and succeed in their academic and social lives.

Gathering the Village

Years ago, teachers and advisors were often expected to be all things to all students. Schools didn't necessarily have counselors or psychologists available day-to-day. Of course, some still don't. While on the one hand, I've designed this book to equip you as a First Responder, in no way should you expect yourself to serve as a de facto child psychologist. My informal saying about teachers and advisors "taking over" counseling students is, "It's all good, until it isn't."

Sometimes a teacher or advisor may believe they can handle a student's needs on their own—or they are expected to do so by their administration. And that might work reasonably well some or even most of the time, until something unexpected comes up that's very far outside the teacher's wheelhouse. The "somethings" I've encountered tend to be a revelation of self-injury or suicidal thoughts (previously non-existent or simply undisclosed) or a complex family situation that may require professional attention.

We know it takes a team to educate a student. It also takes a team to ensure an emotionally healthy school—so students can learn and mature in the most supportive environment possible. No single teacher or administrator has all the information, resources, or strategies to meet the needs of every student. It makes sense for us to pull together and pool our talents. The more urgent or complex the situation, the more important the team approach becomes.

Each adult in a school brings academic and professional preferences and strengths—which is why some of us teach math, some coach tennis, and others counsel students. Each of us also has a particular personal style and way of working. Some of us are better one-to-one, working privately and quietly with individual students who need academic support or personal guidance. Others are ready to speak out, spearhead targeted initiatives, inspire transformation, and drive whole classrooms of kids to new heights. Some of our contributions might come from interests and talents beyond our academic specialties—a Spanish teacher who is also a certified yoga instructor, a mathematician who is an avid hiker, or an English teacher who's a great listener. They might also be identity-based. For example, a Black teacher in a predominantly white school or a gay teacher who is the only adult to whom students feel comfortable discussing questions about their sexual orientation.

Sometimes you won't know how or where you best contribute and support until it happens. A student takes an interest in your advice, your wisdom, your way of being. Or they confide in you for whatever reason about something that really matters. Whatever your talents, your interests, or your skills, fostering collaborative partnerships with skilled colleagues with the aim of producing emotional health, only enables you and the entire school community to better serve students.

Using the Village

While dynamic and resource rich, the group process—as we have all experienced—can sometimes become complicated and dysfunctional. This isn't particular to educational settings, it's a fact of human nature. Knowing this from the start allows us to stay alert to any trouble spots and nurture cohesion and effectiveness by employing the following tips:

Know Who Is on Your Team and Don't Hesitate to Use Them

The team you rely on to help you manage your students' wellbeing and mental health should include teachers, administrators, healthcare professionals, and coaches. When it comes to student mental health, a lot happens in the "gray areas." When you feel, "Someone else needs to know about this," or "I really don't know if I handled that well," or "I just need to talk this through to be sure I understand what is going on here," it helps to be able to turn to someone who knows with the student about whom you're concerned.

The more trusting your relationship with your colleagues, the better and more open your communication will be. This isn't to say these relationships must become personal—professional trust among team members is all that's needed. You can cultivate professional trust by spending time together—for instance, you might eat lunch with colleagues, form a monthly book group, or meet to share pedagogical ideas and strategies. The goal is to build a professional bond strong enough that members feel comfortable with each other.

Pick a Leader or Convener

An effective leader is essential to your team setting goals, making progress, and having productive outcomes. Somebody has to be in charge. So, once you have your team assembled, choose a leader. They don't have to do it forever. Leadership might be revolving—maybe every semester or every academic year. Whatever your group agrees to.

Develop a Working Relationship with Your School's Counseling, Social Work, or Mental Health Professionals

As you put your team together, be sure to make some space for your school's student support professionals. Encourage all team members to be proactive about building a relationship with this counselor or counselors well before they need them.

When I was a school counselor, many teachers made a point to get to know me at faculty meetings. Others actually made appointments for non-urgent consultations about a student's learning style or difficulty making friends.

For me, these conversations and relationships were what made my job feasible and sustainable. As these teachers turned to me for answers and we got to know each other, I looked to them to be my eyes and ears—our school's First Responders—as well as my thought partners. Because of their input, I was better equipped to take care of our students. While I was drawn to my school counselor job because of the kids, I stayed because of the teachers.

Some teachers, however, only came to me in an hour of urgent need—a student became suicidal on a school camping trip, a spurned boyfriend could not give his ex-girlfriend space within our school building, a parent called to say their daughter had just been admitted to a psychiatric hospital, or a student was returning to the classroom after a psychiatric hospitalization—and the teacher wanted to know what to do. As you can imagine, trying to counsel with limited information and time during a crisis situation made my task more difficult. But sometimes, this is how it goes. Some of these predicaments became "bonding experiences" because a colleague and I successfully navigated a major challenge by working together and supporting each other.

Keep in mind that these school counselors and student support professionals are educated, trained, and hired to take care of mental health issues with students. While one message of this book is that you can and should draw on your lived experiences—as a professional, a parent, a once-adolescent—to understand and support your students, it's equally important that you recognize your limits. While I, as a counselor, might be able to help a student with a math equation or an essay, I would hardly expect myself to teach math or writing in place of someone who has spent years training to do so.

Let skilled counselors do their jobs. They know what questions to ask and how to ask them. Don't hesitate to pull in—or at least consult—that professional in your school. But better still, get to know them.

Communicate in Real Time and Real Space

If you're writing more than a couple of emails or texts with team members about a substantive student issue, walk down the hall, pick up the phone, or schedule an in-person meeting. It might seem burdensome, but when it comes to issues of well-being and mental health, there's no substitute for conversation, even if it's over the phone or on Zoom. We as human beings have not mastered establishing or registering tone in email, so discussing sensitive or complex issues by writing notes back and forth can impede progress or resolution. IRL (in real life) communication in this instance is simply more efficient, effective, and accurate.

Discuss Who Reports

When you feel a situation has gotten to the point that you need to contact the school counselor, a senior administrator, or student's family, consider turning to your team to decide who best to report the issue. Sometimes it's obvious. It's your student. It's your classroom. You know the situation best. You report. But sometimes more than one educator has realized something is wrong and has their own experience to share. Sometimes it's not so clear which adult or adults should bring the issue to the administration's, counselor's, or family's attention. When there is a gray area, review with your team who is best suited for the job.

If you're the chosen reporter, it's useful to step back to consider whether you have all the tools, information, and authority or relationships to address the issue fully. Perhaps it would be useful to have another team member with you. This sounds simple, but in real-life, in-the-moment situations, especially when the matter is sensitive or there are privacy concerns, it may not feel straightforward. You want to be able to explain why the issue needs the administration's, counselor's, or family's attention. You also want to be sensitive to the student's privacy.

Relationships are key. The person who reports should be someone who has credibility with the student, someone the student trusts and with whom the student feels comfortable. The messenger is never more important than when working with an adolescent.

Messenger choice is also important for discussing sensitive or difficult matters with parents. Some parents are intimidated by a senior administrator and do better with a more approachable advisor, like a teacher. Still others may be most likely to listen to someone in a position of significant institutional authority.

Adhere to Policy but Don't Become Mired in Precedent

In my experience, public schools tend to be at once bolstered and hampered by established policies and protocols, while independent schools tend to be both bolstered and hampered by a customized, "case-by-case" approach. When it comes to student wellbeing, neither adherence to strict, rigid policy nor a totally customized approach for each student is optimal. In a perfect world, schools can justify decisions and outcomes by pointing to policy and precedent, while also adjusting their approach to fit a particular situation that may be something your school has simply never encountered before.

Student affairs decisions, especially those that involve mental health and wellbeing, benefit from clear policies and procedures with built-in flexibility. To be honest, when I was involved in crafting student affairs policies, it was often the "never before" situations that alerted our team to our need for a clear policy in the first place.

Leadership, counseling staff, and student support teams do their best work and make optimal decisions with a scaffolding in place that provides structure and guidance, and yet allows them to employ their collective judgment. So, make room for both in your operation.

Recognize Your Power and Maintain Professional Boundaries

Perhaps one of the most critical pieces to having an emotionally healthy school is defining and maintaining professional boundaries between students and teachers. Because teachers are stable adults in their students' lives, many students cultivate strong, even emotionally charged, relationships with teachers. This is a normal and typical thing for adolescents to do and—generally speaking—a good thing. Teachers can be wonderful role models, allies, and mentors to adolescents. But when you allow their admiration to go too far, it can be unhealthy for the student. And you. This is even more true when emotional and mental health issues are involved.

For your students, you hold immense power and authority. You appear to them only as a competent professional adult—they don't get to see you burn dinner or swear when you stub your toe. Think back to your middle- or high-school days. Remember your perceptions and impressions of the teachers you liked? And remember how weird it felt when you ran into one of them at the grocery store or maybe the beach? There's a larger-than-life quality that our teachers, especially those we like and admire, tend to take on.

At a public event a few years ago, I was standing in a doorway taking a quick break for some fresh air. A woman entering the building came close to my face as she squeezed through to get inside. When our eyes met, she said, "I know that face. You were in my third-grade class!"

"Mrs. Salk?" I exclaimed. I couldn't believe it.

My third-grade class (well, hers really) was a fifty-student "open classroom" in a suburban public school. In 1975. Clearly a product of its time, in our class, students worked independently at their own pace. I instantly remembered a day when Mrs. Salk stood at the front of the room while we all sat cross-legged on the floor in anticipation for what that day would hold. A classmate asked, "When are we going to learn cursive [writing]?" To which Mrs. Salk quipped, "In about five minutes!" Third-grade me was bowled over with excitement. Mrs. Salk was going to teach me to write like an adult. Needless to say, it was a school year that left quite an impression on me—and Mrs. Salk played a huge role in what made third grade so memorable.

After Mrs. Salk and I chatted for a bit, I boldly asked, "If you don't mind, how old are you? I mean, I'm wondering, how old were you when you were my teacher?"

We figured out that in 1975 she was twenty-six years old. For all third-grade me knew, of course, she could have been forty. Or twenty. It really didn't *matter* how old she was. She was a big deal to me and every other child in that class.

You may not feel like a star, but to some of your students, you are. Adding to their exaggerated notions of you, movies and television series often portray teacher-student relationships that are either borderline or wholly inappropriate by real-life school standards.

Illustrations abound, ranging from the subtle to the egregious. Therapist to a young Matt Damon, a troubled yet gifted young man with a traumatic past. In the 1989 film *Dead Poet's Society* Robin Williams plays is an alumnus-turned-rebel-teacher at boarding school who advises a student to go against his parents' wishes. Spoiler alert: It doesn't go well. A more recent examples is *A Teacher*, the 2020 FX drama television miniseries that glamorizes a sexual relationship between an eighteen-year-old male high-school senior and his young female teacher. In all of these programs, the teacher inappropriately crosses the boundary from professional to personal. That's what creates the tension and drama, of course.

Your students are watching these movies and shows, and others like them: *Gossip Girl*, *Pretty Little Liars*, *Dawson's Creek*, *Riverdale*, the list goes on. And make no mistake, students are getting ideas about the student-teacher relationship from them.

One of my high-school patients watched *Good Will Hunting* (with her father) and regaled me with the details of her favorite scenes. As she enthusiastically recounted a long, dramatic hug between Robin Williams and Matt Damon (therapist/college professor and patient/student), I felt the urge to say, "Yeah, our relationship isn't going to go like that." But I didn't. I kept quiet, knowing that even if she was expressing a (perhaps unconscious) wish that our relationship would be like that, in the end, she would want me to maintain my professional boundaries. Your students will too.

Keeping your teacher-student relationships healthy means establishing and maintaining clear boundaries. And that's not necessarily as easy or as clear-cut as it sounds. Educating adolescents is intense work that routinely requires prompt responses, sometimes under psychological pressure, where the stakes can be high. So, it's no wonder crossing boundaries is easy.

Even responsible, thoughtful teachers can find themselves in interpersonal and moral quandaries as they navigate deeply personal conversations with adolescents. Of course, the boundary crossing that causes the most fear is a sexual or emotionally inappropriate relationship between a teacher and a student. However, keep in mind, that a boundary-crossing situation doesn't need to be that intrusive to cause harm to students.

While it's totally normal for students to become deeply attached to teachers—to rely on them for personal advice and support at times, to look up to them, or even develop crushes on them—it's always the adult's job to keep an eye on the relationship to ensure it's appropriate. You can't control a student's feelings, but you can maintain boundaries for their psychological protection—and your own.

Our schools are required to educate us about professional boundaries annually. While you should pay attention and heed all advice, these presentations can be legalistic, procedural, and dry. Often, they don't consider the nuance of real-world situations. In the end, it's up to you to delineate clear boundaries, maintain them, and revisit them from time to time to ensure they are working well for all involved. This can be a great project for your student support team to work on together. You can educate yourself about student-teacher boundaries. Know which commonly get crossed and how. Train yourself to notice when a relationship with a student moves into dangerous territory.

One "red flag" is when a given relationship becomes more about your own needs than those of your student. Let's say a student confides in you about struggling with their classes, wondering whether they'll ever get a handle on things. They come to you asking what's wrong with them, are they even smart? As they talk, you recall going through something remarkably similar when you were in high school, and you know there were certain strategies that helped you to overcome your difficulties.

Now, it may be appropriate and even helpful (though never necessary or required) to share that you, too, struggled at one point during high school. You might even let your student know what was helpful for you during such a time. This kind of communication offers empathy, as well as practical advice for how to move forward.

However, if you also take this opportunity to share that what most got in your way in high school was a devastating break-up or major depressive episode, that's crossing a line. It's too much information. It shifts the focus to you and your problems. It may also make a student feel burdened, as if they need to care for you.

In a graver vein, when I was a school counselor, I had an eleventh grader whose mother was dying of cancer. The student's

French teacher, well into her sixties, had lost her own father to cancer at exactly the same age. Because the teacher knew the student well and this situation was not only traumatic but highly unusual, she shared the fact of her father's early death with our student and offered empathy.

Before the teacher did so, however, she and I chatted about how it was important that she not "over-share" about her own emotions. She simply stood up as one of the few people—and already an important, admired one—who truly understood the kind of experience few other people in our school had ever endured, and survived it.

All of us are complex emotional beings. Any of us can be drawn in by a student's story or personality—typically in interaction with our own—in ways that may tempt us to do too much or ignore signs that we are crossing boundaries. When possible, self-monitor. But if you find yourself not quite knowing where the boundary lies in a particular situation, consider why this might be. Ideally, run the situation by someone on your student support team, a school counselor, or a supervisor whose judgment you trust, or a mentor outside of your school.

It's not selfish to set limits within a relationship with a student if you believe that doing too much or being too much could lead to something uncomfortable or harmful. Boundaries are important in all relationships—most especially between teachers and students because the power differential is so significant.

Championing an Emotionally Healthy School

By educating yourself about where your students are developmentally, and how mental health issues in adolescents often present—as you have by reading this book—you have put yourself in a better position to manage and affect your adolescent students (no easy feat). You have also learned to recognize which issues and situations might call for professional attention.

Improving wellbeing for your student body means creating pathways throughout your entire school to promote that same understanding of adolescent development and mental health issues. Though you may not be in charge, you and your colleagues do have a say. So, wherever you can—at faculty meetings, annual reviews, or continuing education programs—speak up for the education, the resources, and the policies you now know will create and maintain an emotionally healthy school. If you're so inspired, be a model for your colleagues, students, and administrators by doing all you can to embed awareness, responsiveness, and collaboration regarding issues of mental health into your school culture.

As a teacher, you change lives. Were this not the case, you may well have chosen a different profession. You are on the front line, where the health, safety, social, and political crises of our times intersect. There's never been a more challenging or stressful time to be an educator. Nor a more crucial one.

Talk It Out: A Scenario and Questions for Discussion

Read through the scenario below. Then answer the questions that follow by yourself or with a group of colleagues.

Alex, a tenth grader, is one of the strongest students—and most amazing kids—you've encountered in twenty years of teaching, coaching, and advising. She seems to really enjoy talking with you, not just about classes and basketball (you're her coach) but also "life." Even though she is only fifteen, your conversations can become so deep and meaningful that she seems almost like a colleague rather than a student. In fact, you and she are so much on the same "wavelength" that it seems she can understand things about the school culture that some of your actual colleagues don't even seem to get.

More and more, you find yourself sharing thoughts and musings you've previously kept to yourself with Alex. While it's not totally surprising to you that you can understand and support her with ease, what's much more unusual is how much she seems to understand you.

You now tend to think of Alex first when you see a great movie or read something compelling in the news, or even when you are just feeling a bit down and know that the special connection you have with her will pick you up.

Discussion Questions

1 What's happening for the teacher in this scenario?
2 What's happening for Alex?
3 If you were to find yourself in this situation, what questions would you ask yourself?
4 With whom might you share your experience? Within your school? Outside of your school?
5 What if a colleague confided in you that they were having this kind of experience with a student? What more would you want to know? What would you advise?
6 What should this teacher do? How should they do it so as not to harm Alex or compromise themselves professionally?
7 Is there anything learned from discussing this situation that could become a policy in support of an emotionally healthy school?

Rules for the Road

Let me leave you with these ten quick rules I follow to keep advice to students appropriate, useful, and safe:

1 *Listen.*
2 *Be curious.*
3 *Anticipate being surprised.*
4 *Reflect back what you're hearing and ask clarifying questions.*
5 *Listen some more.*
6 *Be transparent about whether you must tell another adult about something the student has told you ... Let the student know why.*
7 *If it's necessary to loop a parent in, give your student a choice about how you do so. "Would you prefer to talk with your parent(s) first, and then I'll follow up? Or do you want me to just go ahead and get in touch?" If there are two parents, "Which parent would you like me to contact? Does your parent prefer email, or a phone call?"*
8 *Don't keep secrets about a student's safety.*
9 *Don't fly solo. Consult with a trusted colleague or turn to your team.*
10 *Take a deep breath. You've got this.*

DOI: 10.4324/9781003358923-14